ENDORSEMENTS

"Rhonda Rhea lets Scripture enlighten us regarding the real Light and the amazing changes He can make in our lives. Laugh all along the way as you learn to let the changes He makes in you shine for the world to see."—Thelma Wells, DD (Hon.), MMin, president of A Woman of God Ministries

"Rhonda has the unique ability to make the journey of transformation a delightful experience. You are going to love this book!"—Carole Lewis, First Place 4 Health national director

"Rhonda Rhea is the intersection of humor and reality. Rhonda's positive, common-sense, biblical, and honest writing might tickle the funny bone, but it is also sure to encourage the heart and build and strengthen a life."—Pam Farrel, author

"When Rhonda Rhea enters a room, the lights turn on! She exudes energy, joy, encouragement, and hope. Her signature humor and biblical wisdom are perfectly combined in *How Many Lightbulbs Does It Take to Change a Person?* This book will make you laugh out loud while pointing you to a transformed life."—Carol Kent, speaker and author

"Rhonda Rhea sheds biblical light on how to steer clear of darkness and rev up for a spiritual supercharge. In a lighthearted, laugh-yourself-silly way, she reminds us to look to the God of light as our source for a life that really matters."—Allison Bottke, author

"Rhonda Rhea gives us her high-voltage humor along with a biblical charge to look to the light for the power to change, the power to live, the power to grow. Need a life-zap? It's here!"—Patsy Clairmont, author

"A power-packed charge to look to the light of Christ and be changed. Rhonda Rhea has us laughing all along the journey and then uses Scripture as the high beam for our spiritual path. Find yourself laughing in the light!"—Babbie Mason, Dove Award–winning singer/songwriter, author, and TV talk-show host

"Rhonda Rhea makes me laugh. I mean sidesplitting, howling laughter. Then, she makes me think. And she makes me reevaluate. She stirs together a mixture of wit and wisdom that results in life change and real growth."—Jennifer Kennedy Dean, The Praying Life Foundation

"Ever wished you had a guidebook for changing all those difficult people in your life, and make a few changes in your own life as well? Well, here it is fresh from the able and very funny pen of Rhonda Rhea. You'll laugh, you'll cry, you'll give her plan a try!"—Martha Bolton, Emmy-nominated writer and author of 84 books

"Life-changing wisdom illuminated by Rhea's wonderful wit found me turning the pages in anticipation of a much-needed giggle glowing with truth. Rhea's ability to spotlight areas of our lives that need 'enlightening' while remaining self-transparent will encourage every reader, as it did me, to find perfect delight in walking in God's light. This is a perfect reminder for any woman experiencing seasonal transitions . . . change happens but our God remains constant!"—Linda Goldfarb, author, speaker, radio/Web-TV host, founder of Live Powerfully Now Ministries

HOW MANY LIGHTBULBS DOES IT TAKE TO CHANGE A PERSON?

Bright Ideas
for Delightful Transformation

RHONDA RHEA

NEW HOPE
PUBLISHERS
Birmingham Alabama

*Vickie —
You are an
awesome
girlfriend!
Rhonda*

New Hope® Publishers
P. O. Box 12065
Birmingham, AL 35202-2065
www.NewHopeDigital.com
New Hope Publishers is a division of WMU®.

Library of Congress Cataloging-in-Publication Data

Rhea, Rhonda.
  How many lightbulbs does it take to change a person? : bright ideas for delightful transformation / Rhonda Rhea.
    p. cm.
  ISBN 978-1-59669-325-8 (sc)
  1. Christian life. 2. Light--Religious aspects--Christianity. I. Title.
  BV4501.3.R465 2011
  248.4--dc23
                    2011038721

ISBN-10: 1-59669-325-8
ISBN-13: 978-1-59669-325-8
N124132 • 0112 • 3M1

DEDICATION

To my hubs and hero, Richie Rhea,
with love and appreciation.
I can think of no one on this planet
who has shone the light of Jesus into my life
more brightly, more consistently, more lovingly.

CONTENTS

ACKNOWLEDGMENTS

My fam—what an amazing crew! Many thanks to Andy Rhea, Jordan Rhea, Kaley Rhea, Allie Rhea, and Daniel Rhea. Greatest teens and 20-somethings ever. And again, big thank yous to Richie Rhea, my husband, pastor, counselor, encourager, and hero.

My humble and sincere thanks to my prayer team for constantly armoring up and hitting their knees on behalf of my ministry. So much gratitude for the special prayer investment in this project to Janet Bridgeforth, Tina Byus, Diane Campbell, Mary Clark, Theresa Easterday, Chris Hendrickson, Melinda Massey, and Peanuts Rudolph.

Pamela Harty—such a blessing of an agent! Big thanks to Pamela and all those at the Knight Agency who put such muscle and heart into their work to make it possible for me to do what I do.

I so appreciate Andrea Mullins, Joyce Dinkins, Sherry Hunt, and the entire team at New Hope. Thank you for your beautifully surprising servant hearts and for sharing a passion for shining the light of Jesus into our world.

Special thanks to my talented son Andy Rhea (listentothecorners.com) for transparently sharing his songs with such great depth and for allowing me to share with readers from those sweet, deep places the Lord has taken him. And to Jeff Belcher (jeffbelcher.com) for freely sharing from his tender heart for worship and his insight into the Light. So many are blessed by these two!

Kaley Rhea! Awesome test reader/copy editor/idea person/creative consultant/one-liner-generator, and creative writer (kaleyfaithrhea.com). Oh, and also an incredibly awesome daughter. I'm one blessed mama.

More thanks to my church family at Troy First Baptist Church for prayers and encouragement and for seeing every part of my ministry as an extension of our church's ministry.

Additional thank yous to the Advanced Writers and Speakers Association for sharing knowledge, prayers, support, encouragement—with nail, shoe, and hair tips to boot. What a super group of versatile, godly women!

A grateful shout-out to Josh Uecker at New Life 91.9 in Charlotte, North Carolina (newlife919.com), for all the insanely fun radio conversations through all these years—some heavier on the insane side than others—and for giving so much material a sort of test run.

Heartfelt nods of thanks as well to my good friends and coworkers at The Pathway, the Missouri Baptist Convention's official news journal (mbcpathway.com), The St. Louis MetroVoice (metrovoice.net), The Christian Pulse (thechristianpulse.com), Inspire Magazine (inspirestl.com), and Living Light News in Edmonton, Alberta, Canada (livinglightnews.org), for giving me column space for some delicious nonsense in every issue and for kindly supporting me in sharing some of that nonsense in this book.

How did people write books before Panera? Sincere thanks to my personal Panera (known as St. Louis Bread Company in my neck of the woods) in Wentzville, Missouri—my home office away from my home office. I seem to get about a half chapter per cup of your dark roast, a whole chapter with a shot or two of espresso. It's all one sentence, but hey.

INTRODUCTION

ENLIGHTENING STRIKES

You can fool some of the people all of the time. So mostly I like to hang out with those people.

OK, so I guess that's my way of confessing here at the get-go that I'm not always the brightest bulb in the fixture. The other day I thought I had a stroke of genius. Then I realized it was probably just a stroke.

If I do happen to have a big thought, and if it should strike suddenly, could we call that "en-lightning"? A thundering revelation maybe?

In Ephesians 1:18–19, Paul prays for our enlightening:

> "I pray also that the eyes of your heart may be enlightened in order that you may know the hope to which he has called you, the riches of his glorious inheritance in the saints, and his incomparably great power for us who believe. That power is like the working of his mighty strength."

Wow, how's that for an en-lightning bolt!

The Contemporary English Version describes that enlightening as "light" that will "flood your hearts." There is only one way to find understanding and to be able to live the Christian life in successful obedience, and that is to let His light flood our hearts. Fruitful, joy-filled, victorious living happens only as we are spiritually enlightened through the truth of the Word of God and by the inner working of the Spirit of God.

I love the fact that God shines so much of His light through Scripture so that we can see—we can have understanding. There are almost 300 references to light in the Bible, the first in Genesis 1:3 and the last in Revelation 22:5.

In Genesis 1:3 we see light's creation: "And God said, 'Let there be light,' and there was light." It was the very first day of creation. Then in Revelation 22:5 we read, "There will be no more night. They will not need the light of a lamp or the light of the sun, for the Lord God will give them light. And they will reign for ever and ever." From the first chapter of the Bible to the last chapter of the Bible, beginning to end—light!

All of us search for light. We seek enlightenment, understanding, answers. We seek hope. So many people grope through smothering spiritual darkness reaching for something to bring light into their lives. Some even think they've found it in other pursuits. After all, it would be easy for a blind person to think he's found light if he's never seen it or experienced it for himself.

What a privilege it is to look at true light. It's a light that every single person on this planet needs—the real light found in Christ. The real light that *is* Christ. In John 8:12 Jesus says, "I am the light of the world. Whoever follows me will never walk in darkness, but will have the light of life."

Jesus tells us He is the Light of the world, then tells us we are the light of the world (Matthew 5:14). Scripture really is packed with light. We're told to walk in the light, work in the light, look to the light—light, light, and more light!

Our heavenly Father illustrates many things about Himself and about our relationship with Him using light. Light in the Bible often symbolizes the glory of God, His holiness, His wisdom, His favor, and

His direction in our lives. We see His light shining through a burning bush, a pillar of fire, a guiding star, and so much more. Check out the Mount of Transfiguration in Matthew 17, Mark 9, and Luke 9. Glorious!

Are you longing for a change? Are you getting weary in a grisly struggle to change something in particular in your life? Have you fought to change, seen that change occur finally in your life, only to find that it didn't last? Or are there changes you already know you need to make, but you're putting them off, shoving them to the back of your mind?

Then there were those changes that happened whether you were ready or not. Changes that weren't what you had in mind. No minute in life is exactly the same as the one before. Life is in a constant state of flux—a continual newness, every moment changing.

Those kinds of changes are inevitable. Sometimes there's even a choice as to whether the change of the moment will be a good one or a negative one. Do you see yourself making good choices for positive changes? I've heard it said that if you always do what you've always done, then you'll always get what you've always gotten. Progress requires change.

God-given enlightenment brings real change in every way. Lasting change. Reference books call light "luminous, radiant energy." As we look into His light and reflect on His Word, we can't help but get energized!

The God who is powerful enough to create light, then create the sun—the God who keeps the sun blazing and the stars and moon reflecting—that same God is powerful enough, caring enough, and detail-minded enough to light your way. He wants to show you the path of change, to empower that change, and He longs to light the way for you in His magnificent plan for your life.

Thank you, my friends, for stepping into this light journey with me. Let's let Scripture enlighten us regarding real light, and then we can look closely at changes we may need to make to be able to find perfect delight in walking in that light. By His grace and through His working, our lives can be changed—radically changed. We're talking about a stifling-darkness to brilliant-light difference. Then we can look at how to shine that difference so the world can see. And I'm convinced that enlightening can strike even more than twice in the same place.

> *Heavenly Father, I pray for my reader-friend, asking that You will use this book to turn on the light, revealing Yourself in some new and rich way. Father, if there is a need for saving light, I ask that You would grant the faith that's needed and let it shine through Your power and to Your glory. If one is struggling in a dark place, I ask that You would grant enlightenment and new joy. For the one struggling against change, I ask that You would grant comfort, wisdom, trust, peace. Lord, I ask that by the last chapter, each of us will know You better, love You more, and be ever ready to allow You to change us. Like a young plant, I ask that You would cause each of us to grow toward the light. Toward You, You, You! In the powerful name of Your Son, Jesus, our Light, amen.*

PART 1

LIGHTBULB-OVER-THE-HEAD ENLIGHTENMENT

—UNDERSTANDING THE REAL LIGHT OF THE WORLD

GOD IS LIGHT

*"His lightnings enlightened the world: the earth saw, and trembled.
The heavens declare his righteousness, and all the people see his
glory"* (Psalm 97:4, 6 KJV).

I have a terrible memory. So whenever it's time to get a gift for someone, I have a hard time remembering what I've already given them. One friend told me I bought her the same birthday card two years in a row. The exact same card. So embarrassing. And remembering which gifts go where is getting trickier all the time with more people to buy for—and older brain cells to do the buying with.

That's why I was pretty excited when I got an email the other day suggesting a gift that I'm oh so very sure I've never given anyone. It was an advertisement for—are you ready for this?—a gift *defibrillator.* Yeah, nothing says love like a thousand volts to the cardiac muscle! Besides, how fun would it be to get to call in an order for a defibrillator and then tell the person you'd like to "charge it"?

PUT IT ON MY CHARGE

All myocardial infarctions aside, anytime our heart is a little sluggish spiritually, it's unquestionably time to recharge. Clear! And anytime we need a recharge, there's no question who we can run to for that charge. The God of all power. The God who is Light.

Our God is the light of creation, the light that generated salvation, the light who illuminates the way we're to walk, the light that is wisdom, the light that provides, protects, defends, the light that reveals darkness and chases away that darkness, the light that changes us from the inside out. He is the light we are to reflect, the light that indwells us, works through us, loves others through us, forgives others through us, dissipates our fears, grants strength for every challenge. He is the light that shines joy in every circumstance, the light that infuses life with hope. He is the light, the object of our worship, the light that powers us up for enlightened living, the light that teaches us how to deal with darkness and even reveals our own darkness to us. He is the light who changes us and the light who keeps on changing us.

Talk about a gift that keeps on giving!

TAKE ANOTHER LOOK AT THE LIGHT

How great is our God of light! He is the great I Am. He is the God who was in the beginning, is in the present, and always will be in the future. He is the God who created life and the one who sustains it. Is there anyone else we could look to for enlightenment? Is there anyone else who could rightly show us the way? Anyone else who could charge us up to live the life He created us to live?

First John 1:5–7 gives us the light message at full strength:

> "This is the message we have heard from him and declare to you: God is light; in him there is no darkness at all. If we claim to have fellowship with him yet walk in the darkness, we lie and do not live by the truth. But if we walk in the light, as he is in the light, we have fellowship with one another, and the blood of Jesus, his Son, purifies us from all sin."

LIGHTBULB OVER THE HEAD

Ready for some lightbulb-over-the-head enlightenment? Not necessarily the kind that will ensure you never double up on gifts, but the kind that will provide answers for living. True enlightenment comes as we know the God of light better and better, more and more.

Gifts come and go—whether you're giving a gift defibrillator or a do-it-yourself IV kit (another great gift idea—after all, who wouldn't want to be able to start his own saline drip?). We can't begin to imagine the difference the Father makes in our lives as we better understand who He is.

IMAGINE THAT

Did you ever have an imaginary friend when you were little? Since remembering is not my best skill, I can't recall ever having one. I don't think I ever thought of it. If I had, though, since I tend to like an audience entirely too much, I think I probably would've preferred an imaginary *entourage*.

Either way, I'm wondering now if I might've missed some of the magic of childhood. I can definitely see some advantages to an imaginary bud or two. Imaginary friends don't get mad when you forget their birthdays. They don't even have birthdays unless you want them to. They never interrupt. They don't squish you if they sit on your lap. They never argue about which movie to watch. They never argue about anything. And by the way, when you go to the water park, your imaginary friend gets in totally free.

I can see a few limitations, however. Imaginary friends are pretty quiet—definitely not the greatest conversationalists. They're unbelievably slow in taking their turn in checkers. Don't even try double Dutch with your imaginary friends because rope turning is one of their undeniable weaknesses. They can't even single Dutch.

I CAN ONLY IMAGINE

Isn't it sad that a lot of people think of God as sort of an imaginary friend? They think of Him when it suits them and how it suits them. But that's no real concept of our God. He could not be more real. He is the standard for real. He is the one who makes real *real*. He created everything we see and the things we don't see. He created us. And He's not the quiet conversationalist an imaginary friend is. He speaks to us clearly and convincingly through His Word.

In Jeremiah 23:23–24 He says, "'Am I only a God nearby,' declares the Lord, 'and not a God far away? Can anyone hide in secret places so that I cannot see him?' declares the LORD. 'Do not I fill heaven and earth?' declares the LORD."

The Message phrases the last question this way: "Am I not present everywhere, whether seen or unseen?"

No, He is no imaginary friend. Whether we recognize His presence and power or not, He is still present and all-powerful—and He is still all we need. Closing our eyes to the light doesn't mean it's not there, gloriously shining.

POWERING UP OUR THOUGHT LIFE

Why not spend time meditating on who He is, basking in His greatness? We're instructed to ponder, even though we're also told we can never truly grasp His greatness. Psalm 145:3 says, "Great is the Lord and most worthy of praise; his greatness no one can fathom." Even though no one can fathom how truly amazing He is, verse 5 (NLT) says, "I will meditate on your majestic, glorious splendor and your wonderful miracles."

There's enlightening power in meditating on Him and on His goodness. It's in His presence that we find faith, strength, courage, reassurance—and every ounce of power we need for living. Contemplating His presence is like a spiritual defibrillator for every heart!

Pondering the omnipresence of God that He declares to us in Jeremiah 23 is heavy thinking. But it's heavy thinking that causes us to praise God all the more that His omnipresence comes with omnipower. And if we can just imagine a few new words, His omnimercy, omniprovision, omnilove, omni-all!

Let's put that in our hearts—and charge it!

A LITTLE EXTRA LIGHT FOR THE PATH:

"And this is the message [the message of promise] *which we have heard from Him and now are reporting to you: God is Light, and there is no darkness in Him at all* [no, not in any way]. [So] *if we say we are partakers together and enjoy fellowship with Him when we live and move and are walking about in darkness, we are* [both] *speaking falsely and do not live and practice the Truth* [which the Gospel presents]. *But if we* [really] *are living and walking in the Light, as He* [Himself] *is in the Light, we have* [true, unbroken] *fellowship with one another, and the blood of Jesus Christ His Son cleanses* (removes) *us from all sin and guilt* [keeps us cleansed from sin in all its forms and manifestations]."
—1 John 1:5–7 (AMP)

JESUS, THE LIGHT OF THE WORLD

"For God, who said, 'Let light shine out of darkness,' made his light shine in our hearts to give us the light of the knowledge of the glory of God in the face of Christ" (2 Corinthians 4:6).

I'm not usually a late sleeper. If I climb out of bed too late in a day, I get up feeling like I've missed something. The other morning, though, after not sleeping all that well through the night, I slept in until well after eight o'clock. Right, probably not so criminal in the grand scheme of things. I have teenagers who would be extremely unimpressed. In a sleep-off they could outsleep me up one side and down the other. But I still got up feeling instantly behind schedule and a little miffed at myself because of it.

By noon I realized that staying aggravated at myself was making me a little aggravated at everybody else too—magnifying the "annoyance factor"—and frustrating my overwhelming schedule all the more. Is there an opposite for a party attitude?

I did find myself dwelling on skills I wanted to cultivate. But that's not as redeemable as it might sound since the skill I most wanted to develop was that Vulcan nerve-grip-shoulder-squeezy thing. Maybe I get more innovative when I'm annoyed. Not very spiritual, I know. To be perfectly honest, though, I still think the nerve grip could come in pretty handy some days.

GET A GRIP

Anyway, I decided I'd best get a grip (not the Vulcan kind), get over it all, and stop beating myself and everyone else up over not being an early bird. After all, no matter how early that bird gets up, he still ends up eating worms.

A worm breakfast didn't sound good anyway. Me? I'll take coffee, please. And on those kinds of mornings, lots of it. As a matter of fact, I was a bit surprised that particular day that the sun had still come up even though I hadn't made the coffee yet. Who knew?

It also seemed the sun had come up a little on the bright side. As I squinted out the kitchen window, I found I sort of wanted to turn it down a couple of clicks. Eventually I decided instead of turning down the sun, I might do better to turn up the caffeine instead. A two-pot morning for sure. I made a related observation. Sixteen waking hours in a day. Sixteen cups in two pots of coffee. Coincidence? I think not.

ON THE BRIGHTER SIDE

Some days I find myself squinting into the glorious face of God in a little the same way. Not with annoyance or frustration, but with complete awe. It's utterly overwhelming to think that the God of the universe, in the most grace-filled act in all of history, chose to reveal Himself in the light of Jesus Christ, our Savior. His glory, right here on earth as Jesus, the Light of the world! John 1:14 (CEV) tells us:

> "The Word became a human being and lived here with us. We saw his true glory, the glory of the only Son of the Father. From him all the kindness and all the truth of God have come down to us."

Jesus speaks it plainly in John 8:12. Look at it again. He says, "I am the light of the world. Whoever follows me will never walk in darkness, but will have the light of life." In the chapter just before, John tells us that "the Jews' Feast of Tabernacles was at hand" (John 7:2 NKJV). The Feast of Tabernacles was a weeklong celebration of God's provision for the people of Israel when they were wandering in the wilderness. It was a celebration of His deliverance. Jesus gives us another glimpse of Himself as the Messiah who fulfilled all that the feast celebrated.

FEAST ON THIS

During the Feast of the Tabernacles, four huge lamps on poles about 75 feet high were lit in the Court of the Women in the temple every evening. Each pole had four branches and on top of each branch sat an immense bowl. Ten gallons of oil was poured into each bowl. It was said that the light of the giant lamps filled every courtyard in the entire city. What a picture! The light could be seen for miles around. If that wasn't enough light, the people carried torches while they sang, worshipped, praised, and celebrated God the Deliverer with an enthusiastic party-tude—all in the most magnificent light. The light ceremonies of the festival were to remind them of God's Shekinah glory that led them through the wilderness and a reminder of the glory to come. "Shekinah" is the Hebrew expression for the light presence of God.

Jesus declared that He was the Light of the world when this party of light "was at hand." He was, in essence, shining a spotlight on His role as our Messiah/Deliverer. The glory to come. Malachi 4:2 points to Jesus, our Light. "The sun of righteousness will rise with healing in its wings." He shines as the Son-rise to beat all sunrises!

In the Old Testament we read about the coming Messiah who would be a light for His people. Isaiah 60:19 (NKJV) says, "The sun shall no longer be your light by day, Nor for brightness shall the moon give light to you; But the Lord will be to you an everlasting light, And your God your glory."

LIVING IN THE LIGHT OF LIFE

What does this mean for us? How does it change how we think, how we respond, how we live? How does it change how we behave every morning as we get out of bed—whatever time that may be?

Let's zero in on what Jesus says in John 8:12. Those of us who follow Him "will never walk in darkness, but will have the light of life." He delivers a promise with an even wider scope than God's promise of deliverance to the nation of Israel. It's a salvation not just from surrounding enemy nations, but salvation from the darkness of our sin. It's not just a little peek into the light, but an infusion of the righteousness of Christ, our Light. The light of life is a permanent life-fix for those who follow Christ. It's a continuous deliverance for us from the old darkness. And that changes everything. As we surrender our lives to Jesus, we're ushered into this life of great light. New life!

Jesus came to redeem and He changed my life. He changed my destiny from hell to heaven. He changed how I see people and how I behave toward them. He changed how I handle my failures and shortcomings. He changed my world. He changed how I live and Who I live for. And would you believe it, the changes He's made in my life cause me to long for Him to change me all the more. It's true! It all makes me long to know Him better all the time.

NO COMPARE-I-SUN

With every new little thing I learn about Him I'm amazed again. I wonder if God created light to give us the tiniest hint of what He's like. Words can't accurately describe the wonder of Jesus. Words can't even accurately describe light. While we're living in these human bodies, the light of the sun is a bit much to gaze on. These earthly eyes can't handle it.

How much brighter is my Jesus, the high and holy Savior, the Light of the world! In comparison, the sun's got nothin'.

Let's keep on gazing into His light, living in it, focusing on His brightness. Squint or no squint, look up to the Son!

A LITTLE EXTRA LIGHT FOR THE PATH:

"He was with God in the beginning. All things were made by him, and nothing was made without him. In him there was life, and that life was the light of all people. The Light shines in the darkness, and the darkness has not overpowered it. There was a man named John who was sent by God. He came to tell people the truth about the Light so that through him all people could hear about the Light and believe. John was not the Light, but he came to tell people the truth about the Light. The true Light that gives light to all was coming into the world! The Word was in the world, and the world was made by him, but the world did not know him. He came to the world that was his own, but his own people did not accept him. But to all who did accept him and believe in him he gave the right to become children of God."
—John 1:2–12 (NCV)

YOU,
THE LIGHT
OF THE WORLD

"The night is nearly over; the day is almost here. So let us put aside the deeds of darkness and put on the armor of light" (Romans 13:12).

I burned my right index finger on the toaster the other day. Man, did that smart. It might not have been so bad if I hadn't kept aggravating it. Do you know how many moves in everyday life require an uninjured right index finger? It was on the very tip to boot. The typing tip. And I'm a writer. That means every *j, u, n, m, h,* and *y* was painful, not to mention 6 and 7. There are heroic people who deal with real challenges every day, of course—nothing like my wimpy one. The difference is that I'm no hero. I won't even pretend.

That little finger wound not only interfered with typing, but it affected buttoning, stirring, tapping, zipping—poking, picking, pulling, and pinching. It's my lip glossing finger, my microwave button finger, and an absolutely essential part of making that tiny violin motion when I need to let someone know they're whining.

OK, so I'm usually the one who's whining, but think about it. I had to make coffee with only 90 percent of my usual fingerage. Imagine trying to make coffee with that kind of deficiency—without having my coffee first. Tricky. I realized I had barely begun to whine when it came time to do my hair. A hairbrush seems to require at least ten fingers. You might be surprised, too, to find that running your fingers through your hair isn't nearly as satisfying when one of the lead runners is benched.

And what do you do when you eat something finger-licking good but you only get to lick nine out of the ten fingers? You can probably guess just how incomplete that feels. Even button-pushing was hindered. In this day and age, a gal needs her button-pushing finger to be ever operational. It's one thing to have your driving hindered, but I didn't have my radio button-pushing finger. Driving with the radio stuck on a sports show? For me that is really painful.

POINTED REMARKS

At least I could still point with that pointy finger. It's so good that I always have something worthwhile to point out—no fingers required. That something is that everything in life should point to Jesus. If others are not encouraged to look to Jesus by what they observe in my life, there's only one person to blame—all fingers point back to me.

Jesus stepped onto this planet as the Light of the world, crushing the darkness of sin by His redemptive work on the Cross. Then the Light said to us,

> "You are the light of the world. A town built on a hill cannot be hidden. Neither do people light a lamp and put it under a bowl. Instead they put it on its stand, and it gives light to everyone in the house. In the same way, let your light shine before others, that they may see your good deeds and glorify your Father in heaven" (Matthew 5:14–16).

No bowls about it, we've been commissioned to shine His light, all glory pointing to Him!

ALL FINGER-POINTING ASIDE

Not that I'm one to point a finger, but I have to say the disciples weren't looking all that "shiny" just after the Resurrection. In John 20 we're told they were hiding, locked away behind closed doors. A couple of them had seen the empty tomb. Mary told them she had seen Him with her own eyes. Still the door was locked. I might say they were coming down somewhere on the wimpy side if I hadn't already told my wimpy finger boo-boo story.

So what changed the disciples from the wimpy guys hiding in that room into the bold proclaimers of light of the New Testament? John 20:19–22 tells us:

> "On the evening of that first day of the week, when the disciples were together, with the doors locked for fear of the Jewish leaders, Jesus came and stood among them and said, 'Peace be with you!' After he said this, he showed them his hands and side. The disciples were overjoyed when they saw the Lord. Again Jesus said, 'Peace be with you! As the Father has sent me, I am sending you.' And with that he breathed on them and said, 'Receive the Holy Spirit.'"

Jesus didn't leave the disciples to try to muster up some light to shine on their own. He didn't leave them each pointing a finger at the other to go. He commissioned them to shine, and then He gave them His Holy Spirit to empower them to do it.

We have the same Holy Spirit empowering us. Before He ascended into heaven, Jesus commissioned them—and all of us as well—when He said in Acts 1:8, "But you will receive power when the Holy Spirit comes on you; and you will be my witnesses in Jerusalem, and in all Judea and Samaria, and to the ends of the earth."

MORE TO THE POINT

Shining His light is more than just a nice way to live. It's a calling. "But you are a chosen people." You were chosen to tell about the wonderful acts of God, "who called you out of darkness into his wonderful light" (1 Peter 2:9). If you've been called out of darkness and into His light, the calling is yours too. And our Lord will never call you to do anything He won't first empower you to do.

Worship pastor and singer/songwriter Jeff Belcher is on staff at the church my husband pastors. I love worshipping the Light alongside

Jeff. When speaking of shining a changed life to the world, Jeff said, "In Exodus 33 and 34, there is an example of God's glory as radiant light. Moses said to God, 'show me your glory.' He went up on the mountain, spent time with God, and he was allowed to see, not God's face, but His back. Moses didn't know it, but when he came down, his face literally glowed with the radiance of God.

"As we encounter His presence, seeking to give God the glory He deserves, may we be changed so as to shine His light to this dark world."

If my life isn't pointing others to the Lord for His glory and by His glory, my usefulness in life as far as anything truly worthwhile is total toast. *Oh Lord, may I use every ounce of my energy and all the power Your Spirit provides to point others to Your glory.*

His radiant glory. The point of our story.

A LITTLE EXTRA LIGHT FOR THE PATH:

"For you were once darkness, but now you are light in the Lord. Live as children of light (for the fruit of the light consists in all goodness, righteousness and truth) and find out what pleases the Lord. Have nothing to do with the fruitless deeds of darkness, but rather expose them. It is shameful even to mention what the disobedient do in secret. But everything exposed by the light becomes visible—and everything that is illuminated becomes a light. This is why it is said:

"'Wake up, sleeper, rise from the dead, and Christ will shine on you.'

"Be very careful, then, how you live—not as unwise but as wise, making the most of every opportunity, because the days are evil. Therefore do not be foolish, but understand what the Lord's will is. Do not get drunk on wine, which leads to debauchery. Instead, be filled with the Spirit, speaking to one another with psalms, hymns, and songs from the Spirit. Sing and make music from your heart to the Lord, always giving thanks to God the Father for everything, in the name of our Lord Jesus Christ."
—Ephesians 5:8–20

THE LIGHT OF SALVATION

4

"These people who live in darkness will see a great light. They live in a place covered with the shadows of death, but a light will shine on them" (Matthew 4:16 NCV).

I've always wondered why paper beats rock. Because last time I threw a piece of paper at a window? Nothing.

Scissors cut. Rock smashes. I get those. They can do some damage. But I have a hard time feeling all that threatened by a "covering." To me that seems more like…I don't know…getting tucked in. Few crimes are committed by an assailant holding a piece of paper saying, "Don't make me cover you with this." If I had invented the game and wanted to insert something wimpy, I think instead of paper I would've gone with something like "pickle." At least that's a little interesting. And you can eat it.

Excuse me for harping on this one, but when you think about it, even if a paper covering could do damage, if paper can cover rock, why can't it cover scissors? One of life's big questions.

And while we're questioning, I've also wondered why they've never come up with a master item. Like "laser." Or maybe "bazooka." Bazooka annihilates rock, paper, and scissors. And also pickle. Trump!

WHAT A PROVISION

As for our spiritual covering, no need to wonder there. Gotcha covered. If we surrender our lives to Christ, our sin is covered, cut, smashed, and annihilated. Psalm 32:1–2 says, "Blessed is the one whose transgressions are forgiven, whose sins are covered. Blessed is the one whose sin the LORD does not count against them and in whose spirit is no deceit."

People have a tendency to try to cover their sins themselves or to pretend they're not there. Sometimes we like to simply relabel them as little weaknesses or "just part of my personality." But the Bible tells us that there's not a single one of us who doesn't have a sin problem. Have you ever lied? Ever had an impure thought? Ever cheated or stolen or coveted something that wasn't yours? Every one of those goes against God's law. It takes one sin to make you a sinner. Romans 3:23 (NLT) says that "everyone has sinned; we all fall short of God's glorious standard."

A holy God can't have fellowship with sin. And we are a sinful, imperfect, unholy people. The Bible tells us further that the penalty we've earned for our sin is death—separation from our holy God forever. "The wages of sin is death" (Romans 6:23).

WHAT A PICKLE

The pickle of sin is no small thing. Sin entered the world when Adam and Eve chose to disobey God, and we've been living under its curse ever since. Each of us has inherited that sin nature. What does it take to annihilate that sin? Perfection. That really does leave us in a pickle because none of us is perfect.

It's a very sad pickle. So many live a life apart from the Father. The creation separated from the Creator. God places in each of us a longing to know Him and have fellowship with Him. Without that fellowship with our Creator, a person will always feel something is missing from life. And it is. What can a person do? That's life's biggest, most important question of all.

WHAT A PAYMENT

Look at Romans 6:23 in its entirety: "For the wages of sin is death, but the gift of God is eternal life in Christ Jesus our Lord." Our forgiveness was purchased on the Cross of Calvary with the very blood of Jesus.

Romans 5:8 says that, "God demonstrates his own love for us in this: While we were still sinners, Christ died for us." The Perfect One took the punishment so we wouldn't have to. What a payment. The blood of Jesus trumps all!

WHAT A POWER

"You see, at just the right time, when we were still powerless, Christ died for the ungodly" (Romans 5:6).

We are powerless to save ourselves. But Jesus has all power to save. Our salvation is not anything we can earn. It's not a paycheck we receive for living a good life. It's a gift that we receive—a gift that keeps on giving for all eternity. By the power of Jesus, we can have a new standing—one of righteousness—and we can have a right relationship with God our Father. "God made him who had no sin to be sin for us, so that in him we might become the righteousness of God" (2 Corinthians 5:21).

WHAT A PRAYER

If you've never prayed and asked Jesus to forgive your sin and to come into your life, why not let this be your day of salvation? If you can't remember a time when you prayed a prayer surrendering your life to Him, you can clear that up right now. Pray something like this from your heart:

> *Father, I know I've gotten myself into a pickle. I've sinned. I've broken Your laws and I have no hope of living a righteous life on my own. I believe that Your Son, Jesus Christ, came to earth to pay my sin debt and grant me the righteousness I couldn't muster up on my own. I believe He lived a perfect life and then suffered and died on the Cross to pay for everything wrong I've ever done. I believe He rose again three days later, proving He is who He said He was and conquering sin and death once and for all. Will*

You forgive my sin and come into my life? I give You all of me.
Thank You for your forgiveness and for this new life in You. In
Jesus' name, amen.

If you just prayed that prayer for the first time, would you let someone know? Connect with a Jesus follower who can answer some of your questions and help you get started in your new walk with Christ. Get plugged in to a Bible-believing church that can encourage you, teach you, and give you a place to serve. And may I be the first to welcome you into the kingdom of light, my friend. Based on the Word of God, you've just experienced the ultimate change—one you'll never regret.

WHAT A PASSAGE

Jesus describes the change as a night and day, life and death difference. In John 5:24, He says, "Very truly I tell you, whoever hears my word and believes Him who sent me has eternal life and will not be judged but has crossed over from death to life."

How much light is needed to change a person? Only the light of Jesus can change our destiny from hell to heaven. Only by His blood can we pass from sin-covered to forgiven. Only His salvation rescues us from darkness and ushers into a life full of His light!

The change at the very moment of salvation is radical. It's miraculous. He makes everything new. Sin? Annihilated. We're covered by the Rock.

WHAT A PLAN

You don't have to be perfect to follow Christ. He's taken care of the need for perfection. But you do have to be willing to follow the Perfect One with complete abandon. The beauty of salvation is that it's not just about securing a ticket to heaven. It's so much more. God comes near. According to His magnificent, merciful plan, God chooses to indwell your life by His Holy Spirit. There's a new connection. A bond. Life is never the same. He is with you. It's a grand plan—with a party attached!

If it's been awhile since you stepped into that light of salvation, think back to that day you prayed and gave Jesus your all. What a blessed remembering! Celebrate that salvation today. We never tire of hearing His good news, do we? And again, if you haven't yet received the gift of salvation, I hope you will this very day. I guarantee, you'll never be disappointed. "For the Scripture says, 'Whoever believes in him will not be disappointed'" (Romans 10:11 NASB).

Never, ever disappointed.

Which, incidentally, is more than I can say for the rock, paper, scissors game. For instance, if someone throws a rock at your head and you cover your head with paper, I'm telling you, you're going to be sorely disappointed.

A LITTLE EXTRA LIGHT FOR THE PATH:

"How happy is the one whose transgression is forgiven, whose sin is covered! How happy is the man the LORD does not charge with sin, and in whose spirit is no deceit!"
—Psalm 32:1–2 (HCSB)

LIGHT FOR LIVING

"*Light shines in the darkness for the godly*" Psalm 112:4 (NLT).

I opened the door to the microwave to reheat my coffee a few mornings ago then realized I just didn't want to put it in there. Ew. It looked like someone had a tiny little ticker-tape parade. So much food confetti, so little space. Worst of all, there were a couple of spaghetti sauce stalactites just hanging there. Before the coffee was going in, somebody was going to have to clean out that microwave. I like my coffee with lots of sweetener and plenty of creamer. But call me picky, I like it completely without spaghetti sauce drippings.

And speaking of picky, I thought I might actually need a pickax to get to the root of some of those stalactites. Do they make a microwave cleaner that's like plastic explosives? C-4 anyone?

STALAC-STUFF

Life can sometimes be a little like my microwave. Anytime I'm wondering why life doesn't taste as sweet, I really have to look at what I might be hanging onto, stalactite-style. Hanging onto self-centeredness, bitterness, laziness—or anything similar—will zap the deliciousness right out of life.

First Peter 2:1–2 (AMP) gives us a big, ugly list and then tells us that making God's Word a central part of our lives can help us get rid of everything ugly that might be hanging around in there.

> "So be done with every trace of wickedness (depravity, malignity) and all deceit and insincerity (pretense, hypocrisy) and grudges (envy, jealousy) and slander and evil speaking of every kind. Like newborn babies you should crave (thirst for, earnestly desire) the pure (unadulterated) spiritual milk, that by it you may be nurtured and grow unto [completed] salvation."

If you prayed the prayer from the last chapter, giving Jesus control of your life, you may be wondering what's next for you. How should you live now? Or maybe you've been a Christian a long time and still find yourself wondering how to walk it out.

Before we can grab on to what the Lord wants us to do and live this life in the light, and before we can enjoy the satisfaction and joy that comes with fruitfulness, we have to continually let go of sin and selfishness. As we let go of these ugly things, we need to hang on tight to the instruction of His Word, embracing the delicious changes He's making in us.

Have you ever wondered, if we've been redeemed to walk in the light, why then do we still sometimes find ourselves in sin struggles? Since Jesus died for every sin, shouldn't every one of them be forever gone?

THE GIFT THAT KEEPS ON CHANGING

The truth is, at the point you surrendered your life to Christ, you truly were gloriously forgiven. You have a new position in Christ: His. It's a place of sweet freedom from the sin and judgment that was once yours. "Therefore, there is now no condemnation for those who are in Christ Jesus, because through Christ Jesus the law of the Spirit of life set me free from the law of sin and death" (Romans 8:1–2). No more condemnation for you! You are forever and eternally secure as a child of your heavenly Father. But your life is still wrapped in an earthly body, and here on earth the curse of sin still has some sway. There's a battle that rages between your redeemed spirit and your sinful flesh.

But don't worry. You have weapons in this battle. You don't have to fight it in your own strength. You have God's Word. And remember, you have the Holy Spirit living in you, whispering truth into your life and teaching you how to become more like Jesus.

Throughout our time here, our Father is changing us, transforming us into His likeness. Salvation is yours. Done deal. But this transformation, this "sanctification," is a changing process that you will experience for the rest of your earthly life. The more you allow His Spirit to empower you and the more you yield to His whisperings, the more you'll see positive changes in how you act, talk, love, live—shine.

CHANGING IN THE LIGHT OF HIS LOVE

Do embrace those changes He makes in your life. They're a gift of love from a heavenly Father who adores you. And if there are times when you can't feel His love, keep in mind that we can't trust our feelings. We can trust His truth. We can trust the proof of the Cross. We can trust Him.

There are times when people feel unloved because, frankly, they feel unlovable. Focusing on past sins and failures without filtering them through the Cross can do that. Or we compare ourselves with others and see ourselves as those who can never quite measure up on our own scale of spirituality. The enemy loves to perpetuate those feelings. He knows you'll never be able to freely enjoy your walk in the light and reflect that light into the lives of others as long as you're focused on your frustration, guilt, sadness, and hopelessness. Did you know that your Father in heaven never says to a single one of us, "OK, clean up and get your act together so I can love you"? No, His love is based on His goodness, His mercy, and His faithfulness—not on ours.

Anytime you're asking yourself the "What's next for me in my Christian walk?" question, most of your answer is simply knowing that the Lord wants you to experience His love in an intimate, personal, steady way. And He wants to be able to share that love with others through you. He desires to use you to shine His light as you learn to live in it.

PUT ON THE LIGHT

That truly does call us to live consistently in the light. Paul says in Romans 13:12–14 (NLT):

> "The night is almost gone; the day of salvation will soon be here. So remove your dark deeds like dirty clothes, and put on the shining armor of right living. Because we belong to the day, we must live decent lives for all to see. Don't participate in the darkness of wild parties and drunkenness, or in sexual promiscuity and immoral living, or in quarreling and jealousy. Instead, clothe yourself with the presence of the Lord Jesus Christ. And don't let yourself think about ways to indulge your evil desires."

Those are stalactites of the darkest kind.

Clothing ourselves "with the presence of the Lord Jesus Christ" is wearing His light, letting it shine from the inside out. Wearing His presence is being controlled by His Spirit, letting Him rule our hearts and our minds. "Those who are dominated by the sinful nature think about sinful things, but those who are controlled by the Holy Spirit think about things that please the Spirit. So letting your sinful nature control your mind leads to death. But letting the Spirit control your mind leads to life and peace" (Romans 8:5–6 NLT).

Life and peace. To say that walking in the light is a better life is outrageously understated. Letting go of everything stalactite-ish makes sense—even if it does require a touch of spiritual C-4.

A LITTLE EXTRA LIGHT FOR THE PATH:

"And I am convinced and sure of this very thing, that He Who began a good work in you will continue until the day of Jesus Christ [right up to the time of His return], developing [that good work] and perfecting and bringing it to full completion in you.... So that you may surely learn to sense what is vital, and approve and prize what is excellent and of real value [recognizing the highest and the best, and distinguishing the moral differences], and that you may be untainted and pure and unerring and blameless [so that with hearts sincere and certain and unsullied, you may approach] the day of Christ [not stumbling nor causing others to stumble]. May you abound in and be filled with the fruits of righteousness (of right standing with God and right doing) which come through Jesus Christ (the Anointed One), to the honor and praise of God [that His glory may be both manifested and recognized]."
—Philippians 1:6, 10–11 (AMP)

PART 2

BRIGHT IDEAS FOR ENLIGHTENED LIVING

—EMBRACING THE LIGHT OF GODLY LIVING

LIGHT THAT GIVES UNDERSTANDING

"He makes known secrets that are deep and hidden; he knows what is hidden in darkness, and light is all around him"
Daniel 2:22 (NCV).

Just treated myself to a chocolate truffle cookie. It was beautiful. You're probably wondering what occasion would bring on such an enthusiastic choco-celebration. It was my birthday. Well, it was my birthday cookie. My birthday is actually still two months away. But I'm calling it my birthday cookie because life is short. I like to think of mine as more of a "birth-quarter" than a birthday anyway. So let the choco-glut begin.

This mama always says, "Birthdays are like a box of chocolates. You never really know how many you're going to get." I do know, however, about how many of the birthday chocolates I'll be eating. And that would be *all of them*. The orange crèmes don't count, of course. Does anyone really eat those? But everything else that comes my birthday way? Oh yeah. It's going down.

Believe it or not, I'm still on a diet with a 1,100-calorie goal. It's just that during birth-quarter I reach my goal in one cookie. And hey, I'm a goal-oriented person. Give me a goal and I'll try to reach it. Sometimes I reach my day's calorie goal by the end of breakfast.

THE REVENGE OF THE BODY

The diet didn't seem to be working all that well even before birthday season rolled around. Maybe it's related, but I've noticed that when I have to shop for jeans and my diet isn't working, I tend to come home with no jeans and a bad attitude. And also a quart of Ben & Jerry's.

You may be thinking that a person with my kind of diet philosophy will eventually pay. So true. And in so many ways. I think if someone awarded a trophy for the most chocolate consumption, not only should I win the trophy, but that trophy would be made entirely of cellulite.

I sometimes wonder if my body works on other sinister plots of revenge. Several months ago I spent a couple of days in the hospital with kidney stones. Good one, body. I've heard people compare kidney stones with childbirth. Since that stay in the hospital and the experience of having someone drive a tank through my left kidney, I have to say that in a fight, I think kidney stones could so take childbirth. For one thing, with childbirth you come out of the hospital with a baby. Kidney stones? You get to bring home that spit tray thing. No comparison.

COMPARATIVELY SPEAKING

While we're talking "no comparisons," Proverbs 8:10–11 tells us that nothing we desire compares with wisdom. "Choose my instruction instead of silver, knowledge rather than choice gold, for wisdom is more precious than rubies, and nothing you desire can compare with her."

Nope, nothing can compare with the wisdom of God—according to the Proverbs passage, not even silver, gold, or rubies. Not the best jewelry. No matter what we're wearing, when we wrap our minds around His wisdom—and wrap His wisdom around our lives—we simply couldn't look better. Not even with the shiniest of precious stones.

We see the gem of godly wisdom represented in Scripture as light in Daniel 2:22 (NKJV): "He reveals deep and secret things; He knows what is in the darkness, and light dwells with Him."

God is a mystery to us. His light is bigger than we can understand. Yet as we spend time with Him in prayer and in the study of His Word, His Holy Spirit flicks on the light switch, and we can begin to understand more about Him. That increases our faith. And as we mature and our faith grows, He reveals truths about who He is that are deeper still. Remember what Paul prayed in Ephesians 1:18 (CEV): "My prayer is that light will flood your hearts and that you will understand the hope that was given to you when God chose you."

THE CIRCLE OF WISDOM

As we're seeking wisdom, is there anything that can compare to His Word? The more we grow in our knowledge of God's Word, the more we know about our incomparable God and the more we grow in real wisdom. Isn't it wonderful that wisdom leads us to obedience? Then obedience leads us to more wisdom. And the more we grow in wisdom and understanding of our amazing God, the more we are drawn to worship Him. Then Psalm 111:10 tells us that worship is the beginning of wisdom! In the Amplified Bible it says: "The reverent fear and worship of the Lord is the beginning of Wisdom and skill [the preceding and the first essential, the prerequisite and the alphabet]; a good understanding, wisdom, and meaning have all those who do [the will of the Lord]. Their praise of him endures forever."

Did you notice, too, how the circle of wisdom brings us right back to praise? Praises forever to the God of all wisdom! Nothing compares. Not success, not fame, not money or riches—not the most precious gems or even the richest chocolates. Nothing!

Since life truly is short and I don't know exactly how many birthdays I'm going to get, my heart's desire is to use every one of those birthdays wisely. Ephesians 5:15–18 (NASB) gives us a charge:

"Therefore be careful how you walk, not as unwise men but as wise, making the most of your time, because the days are evil. So then do not be foolish, but understand what the will of the Lord is. And do not get drunk with wine, for that is dissipation, but be filled with the Spirit."

YOU DON'T HAVE TO BE A MENSA MEMBER TO HAVE WISDOM

OK, so I guess it wouldn't hurt me to exercise a bit more wisdom in the calorie department either. They say there's a fine line between genius and insanity. I tend to erase the line. And then also erase the genius. Thankfully, wisdom has nothing to do with IQ points. The light of wisdom is realizing we don't have all the answers on our own, admitting we may be doing something wrong, having a willingness to change when we need to, and humbly receiving correction and making the Word of God part of our thinking.

Ask the Lord to open your eyes to His wisdom and to flick on the light of understanding. He desires to show you the riches of His wisdom and to change your thinking in ways that will help you shine and ways that will give you a more satisfying, meaningful life. You'll find your spiritual IQ taking off in new directions.

As for the diet, I read an article the other day that said a big difference between overweight people and thin people is that thin people get an average of two hours more sleep per week. I'm wondering if that means I can eat all the chocolate I want, and then just NAP myself thin.

A LITTLE EXTRA LIGHT FOR THE PATH:

"Your statutes are wonderful; therefore I obey them. The unfolding of your words gives light; it gives understanding to the simple. I open my mouth and pant, longing for your commands. Turn to me and have mercy on me, as you always do to those who love your name. Direct my footsteps according to your word; let no sin rule over me. Redeem me from human oppression, that I may obey your precepts. Make your face shine on your servant and teach me your decrees."
—Psalm 119:129–35

GOD'S WORD GIVES US LIGHT

"The teaching of your word gives light, so even the simple can understand" (Psalm 119:130 NLT).

Have I ever told you about our morbidly obese cat? Whatever it is inside a cat brain that tells the cat belly it's full, it's completely missing from Sammy's anatomy. So he eats and eats until he barfs. Then he moos for more. And I do mean *moos*. Sammy got so fat that we never felt altogether comfortable letting him lean on a load-bearing wall. Fat. Cat.

Several months ago we decided it was time to help Sammy get on a better health track. We ignored the moos more often (difficult though it was—because I mean to tell you, the animal can bellow). We left behind the old feeding system of "mooing for meals." No more wail for it then wolf it down. The "wail and wolf" has given way to a regular feeding schedule. I heard one of the kids telling him, "Just because you can sound like a cow doesn't mean you should end up looking like one." You wouldn't believe how much weight he's dropped the last few months. He's a new cat. Definitely a healthier one.

I'm sad to say, though, that he still looks pretty strange. He's a long-haired cat with all this extra skin that used to be filled with fat. It all sort of sways back and forth when he walks. I can't deny it, it's really gross. When he sits, he sort of "pools" around himself.

The other day we had a little square box sitting in the laundry room, and you know how cats are. He just had to get in it. Well, he sort of "poured" himself in it. And suddenly Sammy was square. Square! It was freaky. He morphed into the shape of the box. I know I'm not exactly one to talk. I've taken a bad morph turn myself here and there. But Sammy. Is. A shape-shifter. Sort of gelatinous, really. Using "cat" and "box" together in a sentence doesn't exactly conjure up warm and fuzzy thoughts anyway, but this was one weird cat box morph.

THINKING OUTSIDE THE CAT BOX

If we're talking spiritual morphs, though, I do hope to transform in better directions. Romans 12:2 is a verse for me: "Do not conform any longer to the pattern of this world, but be transformed by the renewing of your mind."

How do we transform into the right shape and pattern? The verse previous tells us to "make a decisive dedication of your bodies [presenting all your members and faculties] as a living sacrifice, holy (devoted, consecrated) and well pleasing to God, which is your reasonable (rational, intelligent) service and spiritual worship" (Romans 12:1 AMP). We transform as we give it all—every body part (swaying or otherwise), every brain cell, every action, every thought.

As we make that "decisive dedication" Romans 12:1 calls us to, our minds slip into renewal mode and our thinking—our lives—can truly be transformed. Want to become the person you were designed to be? Make the decision to give your all and to let Christ renew your mind through His indwelling presence and through the power-packed truth of His Word.

To be a disciple is to be a student of Christ. But what kind of student never studies? If we want to follow Him well and experience a positive morph, we need to study Him well. We simply can't underestimate the importance of His Word. We need to read it, love it, study it—do it.

BOX YOURSELF IN—IN A GOOD WAY

If you're ready to take some solid steps toward allowing His Word to change your life, let's get a little practical. Check off at least three of these boxes:

❑ If you're not reading daily already, make a commitment to read His Word every single day for two weeks. Pick a special time and place for your daily study, then be flex when you need to. If you miss a day, don't let it frustrate you into chucking the whole plan. That's a win for the enemy. Instead, jump right back in. Ask the Lord to help you keep your commitment and to give you His wisdom in how to order your day.

❑ Set aside some special time this week to take a look at your Bible reading/Bible study plan. See any positive changes you can make? Start a to-do list of new goals for your time in God's Word. Your to-do list might include starting a journal of truths and insights the Lord shows you in your reading—or special words or passages you intend to research or memorize. Pray through your to-do list every day for a week. Ask the Lord to give you all the right to-dos, and then ask Him to empower you to…well…"to-do" them.

❑ If you're not currently in a study, start by finishing this book and digging into its discussion guide. Then ask for Bible study recommendations from your pastor and other godly friends. Ask your girlfriend what she's studying. Search the Internet and ask at your favorite Christian bookstore. There are loads of great resources and study tools available. If it's been awhile since you were involved in a study plan you were excited about, it's time to chase down that topic or book study and dig in.

❑ Find a friend you can make yourself accountable to. We women especially do well to depend on our girlfriends. Ask your friend to check in with you regularly and to encourage you to hold to your commitment. Ask her to pray alongside you that God will give you a hunger and thirst for His Word and that He will help you keep your commitment to read it. Accountability can be such a valuable blessing. At the very same time your friend is encouraging you in your Bible study time, the Lord can also use you as a study catalyst in her life.

❑ Be willing to make sacrifices. To stay faithful in your Bible reading, you may have to give up an activity you enjoy or even give up some extra sleep. It might cost you. But whatever the cost, it's always a good deal. Radical obedience in making His Word part of your every day will result in radical, miraculous, marvelous transformations in your life.

❑ Evaluate again. At the end of two weeks, look back and see what kind of changes your heavenly Father has made in your life. I'm thinking you'll be blown away when you realize what He's done. Notice a renewed life? Praise Him for working in you and for the amazing, life-changing power of His Word.

❑ Make evaluating a lifestyle. Can I just be dirt-dog honest? There are times when my study time is a chore. I don't have the want-to. There's an ebb and flow of my hunger and thirst for God's Word that reminds me now and again that I'm so not where I need to be. I need to be constantly evaluating and reevaluating where I am. I truly want to be constantly morphed into the radiant image of Jesus. That calls me to analyze my spiritual status regularly. When I see a spiritual sag, I know it's time to diligently seek Him, asking Him to renew my fervor. It's His desire that we know Him through His Word. So when we ask Him to renew our passion and our thirst for it, He always answers.

How much light does it take to change a person? A glimpse into the light of His Word can enlighten for a lifetime! The renewed life of Romans 12:2 is not the norm. It's the glorious. And it's definitely living outside the box. This, my friends, is a whole new morph.

So I guess sometimes it's really OK to take a little cue from a gelatinous cat.

A LITTLE EXTRA LIGHT FOR THE PATH:

"Our LORD, you bless everyone who lives right and obeys your Law. You bless all of those who follow your commands from deep in their hearts and who never do wrong or turn from you. You have ordered us always to obey your teachings; I don't ever want to stray from your laws. Thinking about your commands will keep me from doing some foolish thing. I will do right and praise you by learning to respect your perfect laws. I will obey all of them! Don't turn your back on me. Young people can live a clean life by obeying your word. I worship you with all my heart. Don't let me walk away from your commands. I treasure your word above all else; it keeps me from sinning against you. I praise you, LORD! Teach me your laws. With my own mouth, I tell others the laws that you have spoken. Obeying your instructions brings as much happiness as being rich. I will study your teachings and follow your footsteps."

—Psalm 119:1–15 (CEV)

PRAYING IN DE-LIGHT

"GOD *can't stand pious poses, but he delights in genuine prayers*" (Proverbs 15:8 *The Message*).

I'm so glad I'm past the perm days. Remember those days of chicken-fried bangs that look like Velcro? Been there, tried that, fried that.

Actually, being past the perm days merely means that I've found brand-new ways to chicken-fry my hair. Hair color, highlights, flat irons, various other sizzling chemicals and tools—I'm telling you, I usually stay just this side of some kind of hair implosion. Every once in a while I'm just sure I smell smoke.

CHICKEN-FRIED BANGS WITH A SIDE OF HOPE

Here's hoping my perm days are behind me. And while fried bangs may come and go, connecting with our heavenly Father out of love for Him should be a permanent condition. Not "perm with condition," but a permanent condition of seeking Him—a state of ever-light-filled praying. Light-filled praying is faith-filled praying. And faith-filled praying always produces great hope.

Where can you scrape together some extra faith when you're just not feeling it? Romans 10:17 (NKJV) answers, "So then faith comes by hearing, and hearing by the word of God." It comes right back around to staying connected to the Father through His Word. And our faith is strengthened every time we come to Him in prayer.

LOST THAT FAITH FEELING?

Not feeling it? Remember that feelings are unreliable. Faster than hairstyles, they'll come and go. Up one minute, down the next. You can never count on your feelings. You can always count on the Father, the same yesterday, today, and forever.

Sadly, too often we run to our own intellect or experience when we need a shot of faith. It becomes more about seeking self-interest than it does about seeking to become a person of faith. Proverbs 18:2 (HCSB) says, "A fool does not delight in understanding, but only wants to show off his opinions." It's the way our hearts are wired. Jeremiah 17:9 (NKJV) tells us that "the heart is deceitful above all things, And desperately wicked; Who can know it?" How can you trust a lying heart? Feelings can mislead you; don't trust them.

The good news is that you can pray past your lack of faith. In Mark 9 a father brought his demon-possessed son to Jesus for healing. Jesus said, "If you can believe, all things are possible to him who believes" (v. 23 NKJV). The father was in tears when he responded, "Lord, I believe; help my unbelief!" (v. 24). I have to respect that dad's honesty. He readily admitted that his faith was in and out, up and down. He asked the Lord to answer past his wishy-washy faith and to give him the faith he lacked. And how did Jesus answer? He healed the boy! Talk about faith building!

LOOKING FOR LIGHT IN ALL THE WRONG PLACES

It's amazing how those things that are going on in our heads can affect how much of God's message we're able to receive. The right attitude is vital. He resists the proud. James 4:6 says, "God opposes the proud but gives grace to the humble." If we come to our Father with instructions for Him, telling Him what we expect and how we expect it delivered, we shouldn't be surprised when we feel we're not hearing from Him. That's pride-praying, and our Father has spelled out for us that He is opposed to it. How can we expect to see the God of light if we're not even truly looking toward Him? Prideful praying is praying in opposition to Him. It's the exact opposite of seeking Him. If we're looking at what we want instead of seeking His will for us out of love for Him, we'll find ourselves stumbling around in darkness—incommunicado.

James 4:2–3 says, "You do not have, because you do not ask God. When you ask, you do not receive, because you ask with wrong motives, that you may spend what you get on your pleasures."

So how are we to approach Him? Remember these Rs from the Book of James:

> *Respectfully Relinquishing.* If we want to walk in the light, we need to come to Him empty of self-agenda. Come to Him in yielded obedience, humbling yourself before the all-powerful, all-perfect God. James 4:10 gives us the imperative: "Humble yourselves before the Lord, and he will lift you up."

> *Responsively Recognizing.* He desires a sacrifice of praise and thanksgiving. Recognizing all He's done for you is like flicking on a light switch. James 1:17 says, "Every good and perfect gift is from above, coming down from the Father of the heavenly lights, who does not change like shifting shadows." We should respond to all the great blessings our Father of heavenly lights has given us, recognizing every gift is from Him.

> *Radically Relying.* Want to see His light? Trust in Him. We must come to Him in submission, wholeheartedly depending on Him. Trust Him to the point of surrender. James 4:7 instructs to "Submit yourselves, then, to God." We must rely on Him completely, trusting Him to lead us in the right direction.

If we approach our Father—respectfully relinquishing our rights, responsively recognizing His blessing, and radically relying on Him in complete trust—we will hear from Him. He's the Father who loves us. And He loves to answer us. So why strain in the darkness when it's His desire that we understand His will for us? Ask the Lord to line up your heart, soul, and mind to His will. At that place of light-filled prayer, you'll find His perfect direction, you'll find the living hope walking in His will brings, and you'll find all the power you need to walk out your faith in delight.

POWER INAGE

Not long ago we had a power outage that lasted a couple of days. One of those mornings I had an early flight out for a speaking engagement. One of the challenging aspects was that since it was so early, I had to pack in the dark. Scary. I was sincerely hoping I would get to the speaking venue with at least two shoes that matched.

The biggest challenge by far, however, was being forced to get ready *with no blow dryer or curling iron*. Oh, the humanity. It's one thing to go to a speaking engagement with mismatched shoes. But with bad hair? It was so bad that I found myself dreaming of the days of perm-induced chicken-fried bangs. I was sorely—and follicly—missing the power.

It was a good reminder, though, that a power outage doesn't have to be our biggest worry. Why? Because we have a power "inage." When we have Jesus on the inside, we have all the power we need to walk in the light and live a life of real significance. Colossians 2:9–10 says:

> "For in Christ all the fullness of the Deity lives in bodily form, and you have been given fullness in Christ, who is the head over every power and authority."

He is the head of every power, and we've been fully given His fullness. That's a lot of "full." Could we even get any more power-full?

I'm so thankful to the God of all power who has, by His grace, allowed the fullness of His power to live in us through His Son, Jesus. And by that same grace, we can come to the Father through His Son and get all the more powered up in prayer. A powerful prayer life is the way to live in delight. And in "the" light. With or without electricity. Even with or without good hair.

A LITTLE EXTRA LIGHT FOR THE PATH:

"Please, LORD, hear my prayer and give me the understanding that comes from your word. Listen to my concerns and keep me safe, just as you have promised. If you will teach me your laws, I will praise you and sing about your promise, because all of your teachings are what they ought to be. Be ready to protect me because I have chosen to obey your laws. I am waiting for you to save me, LORD. Your Law makes me happy."

—Psalm 119:169–74 (CEV)

BELIEVERS
WHO REFLECT

"Even in darkness light dawns for the upright, for those who are gracious and compassionate and righteous" (Psalm 112:4).

I confess I don't have the greenest thumb on the block. As a matter of fact, I was thinking it might be easier to just give up on all other greenery and grow a poison ivy garden instead. Even for that I'd have to start from scratch.

Scratch? Get it?

Anyway, I decided it would probably be better not do anything that "rash."

SCRATCHING WHERE IT ITCHES

We really do have to be careful what we plant, though. We will reap what we sow. It's right there in Galatians 6:7. And according to the verse that follows, not only should we be careful what we plant, but we're told if we choose to live only to please our own sinful selves, we'll reap a harvest of death and decay. I think I've grown that kind of plant before. But when we're talking about what we're growing spiritually, we're talking about an especially ugly garden. Eternally worse than poison ivy. Don't even bother with the weed-whacker. Roundup won't cut it either.

Take a look at the passage:

> "Don't be misled—you cannot mock the justice of God. You will always harvest what you plant. Those who live only to satisfy their own sinful nature will harvest decay and death from that sinful nature. But those who live to please the Spirit will harvest everlasting life from the Spirit. So let's not get tired of doing what is good. At just the right time we will reap a harvest of blessing if we don't give up. Therefore, whenever we have the opportunity, we should do good to everyone—especially to those in the family of faith" (Galatians 6:7–10 NLT).

KEEP ON REFLECTING THE LIGHT

I love how Paul rounds out his point in verse 9 with the big "so." "So let's not get tired of doing what is good." He lets us know that harvest thinking and learning to live to please the Spirit instead of the flesh leads to staying energized in doing good things for the kingdom. That, my friends, is reflecting the light of the Lord, and it leads to a harvest of everlasting blessing.

Our gardening time here is short. We need to stay on task. 2 Timothy 4:2–5 charges us to:

> "Preach the Word; be prepared in season and out of season; correct, rebuke and encourage—with great patience and careful instruction. For the time will come when men will not put up with sound doctrine. Instead, to suit their own desires, they will gather around them a great number of teachers to say what their itching ears want to hear. They will turn their ears away from the truth and turn aside to myths. But you, keep your head in all situations, endure hardship, do the work of an evangelist, discharge all the duties of your ministry."

Instead of catering to the poison-ivy-itchy-ears of those who simply want the easy way, and instead of letting them distract us, we're called to keep our heads and to steadfastly continue working in whatever ministry God has called us to. We're called to reflect the light of His love by serving others. The passages in Galatians 6 and 2 Timothy 4 are the kinds of sound-the-charge verses we can put to memory (you may need "scratch paper"). They can remind us all along the way to stay tenaciously resolute in our service. It's then that we can become the kind of Christ followers who don't just tickle itchy ears but truly scratch those eternal itches, reflecting Christ's love and patience.

REFLECTING MORE ON LOVE AND PATIENCE

Isn't it amazing how some people know just how to find our weak areas in the patience department? They find our anger buttons…and then they jump up and down on them.

I thought about giving somebody a piece of my mind the other day. Then I thought, "Know what? I really can't spare it!" I tend to suffer a bit of a brain cell shortage as it is. Why should I give any away? I need all I've got!

I don't wonder for a second why there's so much in the Bible about relationships—heavy on the patience and forbearing and forgiveness and the go-the-extra-mile reflecting kind of love. I think so much of Scripture is dedicated to relationships because our heavenly Father knows they can be oh-so hard. Let's face it, people can be jerky. And even when they're not, sometimes I am.

PIECE OF MY MIND VERSUS PEACE OF MIND

It's our Father's desire that we reflect His love by loving each other. It's our calling. Jesus says in John 13:34–35:

> "A new command I give you: Love one another. As I have loved you, so you must love one another. By this all men will know that you are my disciples, if you love one another."

Jesus gives it in the form of a command, not as a suggestion. And according to our Savior Himself, we wear our love for each other as a shiny Disciple ID badge. We can show the world that Jesus makes a difference in our lives.

It does require extra humility and patience. But there's nothing like living in obedience and living in a way that promotes peace with God's people. Paul instructs in Ephesians 4:2–3, "Be completely humble and gentle; be patient, bearing with one another in love. Make every effort to keep the unity of the Spirit through the bond of peace." Hmm. Peace of mind instead of a piece of my mind. Not a bad trade.

Sometimes loving others involves getting rid of our own bad habits, impatient attitudes, and short fuses. Ephesians 4:31–32 spells it out: "Get rid of all bitterness, rage and anger, brawling and slander, along with every form of malice. Be kind and compassionate to one another, forgiving each other, just as in Christ God forgave you."

Difficult? Sometimes. But we have not only the forgiveness of God as our inspiration and the life of Christ as our example, we also have the Holy Spirit living inside us, giving us everything we need to love others in His name. There's hardly anything sweeter than enjoying obedience and the sweet bond of peace he gives when we love His people.

"Losing my mind" is one thing. But giving someone a piece of my mind? That makes less sense all the time. I'm asking the Lord to constantly change me into a believer who mirrors His love, reflecting His light more all the time. I'm even asking Him to help me become more plantlike—constantly growing toward the light of the Son.

BUT WAIT! THERE'S MORE!

I've sometimes wondered if I have all that trouble with my plants because I'm not using the right tools. There are gadgets on TV commercials that are supposed to basically grow the entire garden for you. Take some seeds, add their handy-dandy miracle tool, and voila! Instant gorgeous foliage. They show the big, flourishing plants on TV. That's proof it works, right? Because it's on TV.

I also saw a knife advertised on TV. I thought that any kitchen knife that could cut through the fender of a Buick and still make beautiful carrot curls would certainly turn me into a better cook. Perhaps even a better person. The people on the commercial practically guaranteed it.

The problem was that when I got it, I needed the knife to get the knife out of the package. What's up with that megaplastic stuff? It's impenetrable. Stronger than the shields on the Starship Enterprise. I used scissors and an older knife. And possibly the can opener at one point. I finally got an edge of the package cracked. Shields down to 98 percent. It took another 20 minutes to open another edge. Shields still holding. By the time I got all the way in and started working on the 50-gauge wire that tied it down, I needed a shower, a strong cup of coffee, and maybe a couple of stitches.

TOOLS FOR REFLECTING HIS LIGHT

There are practical tools for reflecting His light that are easier to get to. They're in God's Word. We need to make sure that we're altogether open to picking up these tools and using them in our own spiritual gardening. The last thing we want to do is to put up barriers that could block out His reflection.

Among these tools is remembering not to try to reflect your own love. It's only in Him and through Him that we can love well. Trying to grow it on our own will never yield any kind of lasting results. No real roots there. Paul tells us in Colossians 2:6–7 (NCV), "As you received Christ Jesus the Lord, so continue to live in him. Keep your roots deep in him and have your lives built on him."

It might not seem like a tool, but another important aspect of becoming an effective light reflector is the uniform. There are over a dozen tools in the "what to wear" passage of Colossians 3:12–17. Take a look at it in the "A Little Extra Light for the Path" for this chapter. Among the perfect tools are mercy, kindness, humility, gentleness, patience, forgiveness, thankfulness, wisdom, and praise—all wrapped in love.

O Lord, equip us to reflect Your glorious love. Let us grow in the area of loving people, reflecting the light of Your Son. May we grow as a healthy plant grows, ever-reaching toward the light.

A LITTLE EXTRA LIGHT FOR THE PATH:

"God has chosen you and made you his holy people. He loves you. So you should always clothe yourselves with mercy, kindness, humility, gentleness, and patience. Bear with each other, and forgive each other. If someone does wrong to you, forgive that person because the Lord forgave you. Even more than all this, clothe yourself in love. Love is what holds you all together in perfect unity. Let the peace that Christ gives control your thinking, because you were all called together in one body to have peace. Always be thankful. Let the teaching of Christ live in you richly. Use all wisdom to teach and instruct each other by singing psalms, hymns, and spiritual songs with thankfulness in your hearts to God. Everything you do or say should be done to obey Jesus your Lord. And in all you do, give thanks to God the Father through Jesus."

—Colossians 3:12–17 (NCV)

LIVING SAFELY IN THE LIGHT

"Lord, lift up the light of Your countenance upon us"
(Psalm 4:6 NKJV).

Have you ever had one of those frightening experiences where you were in such mortal danger that you saw your life flash before your eyes? I've experienced fear, but I guess I've never been near enough death to get to see the show.

In our society, we're so used to being entertained that I wonder if any of us would actually walk out on our own life movie. What if the main characters are just not strong enough to carry the story? Or what if the plot slows in the middle? What if your blooper reel is considerably more entertaining than the life show itself? That's a scary thought. Not near-death-let's-see-the-whole-life kind of scary. But scary enough.

If my life ever does flash before my eyes, I'm actually thinking that it would probably be a sitcom.

DELIGHT IN "THE" LIGHT

Still, every once in a while, I have to make myself look at the plot. When I look plot-ward, do I see substance? Something worth living for? Something worth dying for? Am I allowing the perfection of the

Lord to overcome any distress, to be my comfort and to give my life real and eternal meaning?

David was known for being a man after God's own heart. Not because he lived a perfect life. The sins he committed are still considered "the biggies." No doubt his life-flash would not have been pretty. It wasn't his sinlessness that won him the title of God's heart guy. It was more about where he ultimately kept his priorities. "The one thing I ask of the LORD—the thing I seek most—is to live in the house of the LORD all the days of my life, delighting in the LORD's perfections and meditating in his Temple. For he will conceal me there when troubles come; he will hide me in his sanctuary. He will place me out of reach on a high rock" (Psalm 27:4–5 NLT).

David's number one all-consuming desire was to live in the Lord's house every day—to delight in Him. To live in His house refers to dwelling with Him, living in the light of His presence, day by day, moment by moment.

DELIGHTFULLY SAFE

When delighting in His presence becomes the one thing we seek the very most—when it becomes what our life movie is all about—we find ourselves living in a kind of safety we can know in no other place. Where does He hide us? In His sanctuary. His safe place. Is there any place safer than this, our very Creator's place of loving shelter?

Living in that safe place doesn't necessarily mean we won't experience difficulty. But it does mean that there is no difficulty or danger, near-death or otherwise, that can threaten our real security. Our souls are eternally safely nestled away in our Father's protection. It's the place of no worries. "Out of reach," the passage says. Our Father will never allow anything to happen to us that's not for our ultimate good. Nothing. Your worst enemy's plot against you? That's the kind of movie you can walk out on. Their schemes are nothing when compared to the God who holds you, loves you, and protects you. "God has said, 'Never will I leave you; never will I forsake you.' So we say with confidence, 'The Lord is my helper; I will not be afraid. What can mere mortals do to me?'" (Hebrews 13:5–6). Even in painful places, never doubt His presence, His love, and His eternal provision for you.

STAYING ON TRACK

Every once in a while, when I slip into worry mode instead of finding comfort in trusting in the God who protects, I have to ponder my life movie again. It's at those times I think my life could really use a laugh track. Every place I need to lighten up and realize He's got me covered in the most joyful way? Insert canned laughter! A spontaneous song and dance number here or there would probably be a little over the top, but I wouldn't mind having background music. Maybe even a theme song. But what rhymes with "ridiculous"?

For the record, I doubt I would ever be allowed to write my own life story's theme song. Poetry is not exactly my strong suit. In case you need proof, here's my lotion poem:

Got some new lotion
It's like lard for my hands
Gotta be one of my favorite brands

I know what you're thinking. That didn't exactly bring a tear to your eye, and you're wondering why I would waste time on it. I wrote it for one reason and one reason only. And that was so I could call it "poetry in lotion."

FROM BAD TO VERSE

I'm sure you need no more proof, but just in case, here's one called "Another Poem by Rhonda Rhea." Read it only if you're of strong literary constitution:

I love writing poetry
Each phrase rhyming sweet
I love writing poetry
But I'm not very good at it.

Clearly the poets who edit, revise, and dissect their poems to perfection would simply dissect mine. I'm not a poet, and I'm comfortable with that. But while I'm comfortable with who I'm not, I'm even more comfortable with who my God is. I take great comfort in knowing that He is Jehovah Shammah, "The God Who Is There." That means every time I forget that He's got my kids covered, for instance—even when they're scattered all over the world—I must rein in the worry and simply "know." I know that "The God Who Is There" is just as "there" wherever my children are serving as He is "there" when He is here with me. Don't try to diagram that sentence. It might fight you. No need to diagram it anyway; just believe it. It will draw you straight into the light of His comfort.

Psalm 31:20 (NLT) says, "You hide them in the shelter of your presence, safe from those who conspire against them. You shelter them in your presence, far from accusing tongues." The Father protects by His very presence. In His presence, there is perfect safety.

SO MUCH LIGHT. SO MUCH COMFORT

It's also comforting to me when I consider that my God, the light of life, has my story—accompanying songs, poetry, and all—in His prevailing hands. I'm praying that via His comfort, I'll be able to shine all the more, and that if my life ever does flash before my eyes, it will be more like a light show.

The story—beginning, middle, and end—really has to be all about Jesus. He's the heart of every blessed story. He's even our happy ending. Keeping our eyes on Him, if we make it to that life-flash screening, it just might turn into a movie we'll enjoy watching. Maybe we'll even find ourselves bringing popcorn, Diet Coke, and an extra large box of Junior Mints.

Then again, instead of waiting for the life-flashing-before-my-eyes movie, maybe I should go ahead and write my autobiography. I'm thinking of doing it as a pop-up book.

A LITTLE EXTRA LIGHT FOR THE PATH:

"The Lord your God is with you.

He is mighty enough to save you.

He will take great delight in you.

The quietness of his love will calm you down.

He will sing with joy because of you."

—Zephaniah 3:17 (NIrV)

PART 3

SEEING YOUR LIFE CHANGE—ONE WATT AT A TIME

—WALKING IN THE LIGHT REQUIRES OBEDIENCE

STEERING CLEAR
OF DARKNESS—SIN

"Blessed are those who have learned to acclaim you, who walk in the light of your presence, LORD" (Psalm 89:15).

Not long ago somebody gave me a big box of chocolates. I was so excited. Chocolates, man. It was one of those boxes of chocolates with the map in the lid. To me? That lid diagram is a treasure map. There are times when there's nothing sweeter than digging for treasure.

But then something really awful happened. I got sidetracked and forgot to take the box out of the car. A few hours baking in the car and instead of a box of chocolates, I ended up with a chocolate ooze that eventually resolidified into one giant chocolate. There's a lesson learned—a tough one. I'm tearing up just thinking about it. It's just too sad when good chocolate goes bad. Treasure lost.

Spiritual lessons are a much greater treasure. Learning on the spiritual side should always be based in God's truth. And anytime we refuse to learn, we have to go another round with that lesson. More melted chocolate. Now that gets messy.

RESOLIDIFYING

How it must break the heart of God when we get messy, slow to learn spiritual lessons—when we're so slow to obey His Word.

First Peter 1:13–14 says:

> "Therefore, prepare your minds for action; be self-controlled; set your hope fully on the grace to be given you when Jesus Christ is revealed. As obedient children, do not conform to the evil desires you had when you lived in ignorance."

How often do we forget about self-control and turn back to that old way, conforming to the evil desires we had when we lived in ignorance? Why do we even look back at the darkness once we've seen the light?

Are you ready to take action? Is it time for a change? Are you ready to commit to learning whatever your Father wants you to learn? Are you ready to choose obedience? Ready to commit to right choices? Time to resolidify.

Ask the Lord to open your eyes to the old paths of sin. Sometimes those old paths are well-worn and easy to slip back onto. Ask Him to give you the wisdom to choose well. You can. You can choose well, even without a map in the lid. Remember, when you ask for wisdom, He will answer.

WALKING IN THE LIGHT SO WE DON'T STUMBLE OVER "THINGS"

It's all too easy to treasure the things of the world and miss the treasures of heaven—especially when we're hearing from all directions that wealth equals success. The truth is, success is becoming who God wants you to become and reflecting His light in this world. Paul says in 1 Corinthians 7:31–32 (NLT):

> "Those who use the things of the world should not become attached to them. For this world as we know it will soon pass away. I want you to be free from the concerns of this life."

It's not wrong to make good use of what we've been given. We are to appreciate things, use things, enjoy things, but never, ever cling to things. We're wise when we invest our all in eternal treasure and not the temporary trappings that threaten to steal away our focus.

First Timothy 6:17–19 (NLT) gives us such great perspective:

"Teach those who are rich in this world not to be proud and not to trust in their money, which is so unreliable. Their trust should be in God, who richly gives us all we need for our enjoyment. Tell them to use their money to do good. They should be rich in good works and generous to those in need, always being ready to share with others. By doing this they will be storing up their treasure as a good foundation for the future so that they may experience true life."

If you're struggling in the area of clinging to and treasuring money or the things it can buy, bring it all before the Lord as well. Ask Him to help you remember which things are temporary and which will last. Ask Him to give you the discernment you need to stay free from any unnecessary "concerns of this life."

THIS IS WORTH REPEATING

My daughter Kaley has always been one of those blessed totally compliant children. She's 21 now. But I remember a few years ago when she was still in high school, I told her how much I appreciated her consistent, obedient spirit. I said, "You know, Kaley, I think about the most rebellious thing you've ever done is to lather, rinse, and NOT repeat."

She laughed and then after a pause, she said, "Wait. You're supposed to repeat every time? If you need me, I'll be in the shower."

Funny, yes, but I could surely learn a lesson or two from that girl. Instant obedience. That's what the Lord wants from His children.

There is such blessed delight in the life of one who doesn't just read the truth or simply know the truth, but the one who obeys it. Take a look at how *The Message* phrases James 1:22–25:

"Don't fool yourself into thinking that you are a listener when you are anything but, letting the Word go in one ear and out the other. Act on what you hear! Those who hear and don't act are like those who glance in the mirror, walk away, and two minutes later have no idea who they are, what they look like. "But whoever catches a glimpse of the revealed counsel of God—the free life!—even out of the corner of his eye, and sticks with it, is no distracted scatterbrain but a man or woman of action. That person will find delight and affirmation in the action."

Looking for delight and affirmation? Looking for an end to the dark, disconnected, messy, scatterbrained life? Find it in acting in obedience. That's something that will always be worth repeating—even if you never lather or rinse.

NO REGRETS

You will never regret one act of obedience. Likewise, no single act of disobedience will bring satisfaction and lasting joy. And it's not just the big acts of obedience. Every time you obey a command in His Word, every time you get a nudge from the Holy Spirit and act on it—even if it's a small thing—you're blessing your Father. And that's certainly no small thing. Additionally, obeying Him in the small things will lead you to obey Him in the bigger things.

In the fifth chapter of Luke, Jesus told Peter to put his boat into deeper water and let down the nets to catch some fish. Peter said to Him, "Master…we've worked hard all night long and caught nothing! But at Your word, I'll let down the nets" (Luke 5:5 HCSB).

I can't imagine fishing all night long, hour after hour, and all for nothing. Peter had to have been tired and frustrated. And Jesus asked him to let down the nets again? Again? Really? Still, though I doubt Peter's heart was completely into fishing at that moment, he obeyed his Lord.

"When they did this, they caught a great number of fish, and their nets began to tear. So they signaled to their partners in the other boat to come and help them; they came and filled both boats so full that they began to sink" (Luke 5:6–7 HCSB). Talk about a boatload of blessing!

GOING DEEPER

Ready for some deeper water? Obey Him, even when what He's asking of you might not seem logical. Even if you think it might not work. Even if you're tired. Even if you'd really rather go a different direction. Even if you've tried it before. Obey Him, and He will bring in the fish. Blessings will fill your net. Fill your boat. Fill TWO boats. And more! There is always blessing in obedience. We're talking about real treasure!

There really is treasure in obedience—and in leaning on Jesus, loving Him, serving Him, bringing glory to His name. The most precious treasure is Christ. Paul tells us in Colossians 2:2–3 that he wants us to have full confidence in complete understanding of God's plan. What is God's plan? Our richest treasure, Christ Himself! "In him lie hidden all the treasures of wisdom and knowledge" (Colossians 2:3 NLT).

So let's treasure Christ with our obedience, steer clear of darkness, and enjoy the blessings we find in His light.

Speaking of blessings, I have to say that I discovered a silver lining in the chocolate-melting incident in my car. Now that it's one big hunk, I can eat the whole pound and still tell people I only had one piece.

A LITTLE EXTRA LIGHT FOR THE PATH:

"Don't store treasures for yourselves here on earth where moths and rust will destroy them and thieves can break in and steal them. But store your treasures in heaven where they cannot be destroyed by moths or rust and where thieves cannot break in and steal them. Your heart will be where your treasure is."
—Matthew 6:19–21 (NCV)

SOMETIMES THE KEY TO CHANGE IS...CHANGE

"And he [Jesus] said: 'Truly I tell you, unless you change and become like little children, you will never enter the kingdom of heaven'" (Matthew 18:3).

Change can be tough. Most years I have such a difficult time merely shifting between the seasons that my gears sort of start to grind. It's especially tricky toward the end of the year when I lose track of which calendar event I'm supposed to be celebrating. I'm not one to celebrate Halloween, but hey, I eat the candy. What kind of person turns down a Butterfinger?

While we're talking about those Butterfingers, though, I have to say that I'm not sure I'll ever understand why they call that little tiny, half-a-bite-thing "fun size." Show me a quarter-pounder Butterfinger and I'll show you some real fun. A party!

But before a person can even get to the party, we've shifted gears and moved into the Thanksgiving pumpkin pie season. That season leads handily into the Christmas pumpkin pie season. At least we get a couple of seasons out of the pie. I guess it just proves that eating pumpkin pie is habit-forming. If they ever come up with some sort of aid to help us quit, I hope they call it "the pumpkin patch." Wouldn't that be funny? Then at least I'd get a chuckle out of all the extra calories.

No wonder my gears are grinding. And also, no wonder my thighs are sparking.

Shifting gears doesn't really have to grind—not if we make sure we're walking in the light of Jesus in every season. Every day of our lives brings a new change of some kind or another. So many people in this life seem to only like change if it's coming out of a candy machine. If you haven't seen anyone freak out over change in a while, just log onto Facebook the day after some sort of redo in the layout of the profile pages and watch the e-mayhem. Rioting in the cyberstreets! I've wondered a couple of times if we should form some sort of wireless National Guard.

CHANGING OF THE GUARD

I hope this doesn't sound disrespectful, but wouldn't it be nice if every time the Father was ready to bring about a big change in our lives, He asked us what we thought about it first? That's how it would probably work if He didn't have a plan. He does have a plan, though. And it's a good one. "'For I know the plans I have for you,' declares the LORD, 'plans to prosper you and not to harm you, plans to give you hope and a future'" (Jeremiah 29:11). His is a plan that's bigger than whatever we might think of His change.

If we're wise, we'll come to embrace the idea that our plans need to line up with His—not the other way around. Peter, James, John, and Andrew were fishermen before Jesus called them to follow Him. It was a job that consumed much of their thinking and most of their days. When Jesus said, "Follow me," everything changed dramatically. Everything.

Their means of providing for themselves financially changed. The people they spent time with changed. Their lifestyles. Their daily duties. Their loves. Changed, changed, changed. Eventually the very reason they lived out each day changed.

Sometimes the Lord requires us to make changes. Sometimes gloriously blessed changes. Sometimes very difficult ones. They might be job changes, changes in relationships, financial changes, changes in entertainment or habits. But at the foot of each change is an opportunity for us to align our plans with His. And that's exactly what He calls us to do.

Happily, every sacrificial change He asks of us is truly for our ultimate good. Jesus says, "And everyone who has left houses or brothers or sisters or father or mother or wife or children or fields for my sake will receive a hundred times as much and will inherit eternal life" (Matthew 19:29). He is a perfect, gracious, merciful, loving God, and we can trust Him. We can trust Him even when the changes are painful. He sees the big picture.

CHANGING MY MIND

Walking in His light requires a change in the way we think. At the point we surrender our lives and our minds to Christ, we're set free from the power of sin that was once our master. We're free to choose light. We can pursue a godly walk.

As we filter our choices through the Word of God, continually lining up our thinking with His, we can more easily reject ungodly, unhealthy thoughts. As we develop habits of godly living, our minds become more in tune with His, and we reflect Him more and more. His Spirit nudges us when our thoughts need to change. As selfishness, worry, rebellion, and other impure thoughts creep in, by His Spirit, He gives us everything we need to shift gears. We're fully His. And we're never the same.

My oldest son is a wonderful songwriter and musician. He wrote a poem called "We'll Never Be the Same," based on an analogy of God—our Light—as cleansing fire. When Andy and I were talking about this poem, he mentioned how God-our-fire destroys and refines and cleanses. He said the last stanza in the poem is about how we can help the fire become brighter as we surrender, consumed by the fire. And though every element in the fire is transformed, the fire itself is always the same element.

We'll Never Be the Same
—by Andy Rhea (used by permission)

There's fire washing up the shore
A ceaseless flowing mass
It bends the palm trees to their knees
And turns the sand to glass

The dancing embers bring the laud
The dead things fuel the flame
The lupines glow. Transformed, they sing,
"We'll never be the same.
We'll never be the same.
Though naked now,
We have no shame.
We'll never be the same."

There's fire crashing past the shore
And down the darkest streets
The prison bars surrender debts
And crumble from the heat

And when it seems the presence of
The flame might dissipate
The trees give air, the air combusts
They all participate

The trees to air to light to logs
The fellowship, the bond
The fire stays the same and so
Our King, His crown is dawned

MY CONSUMING PRAYER

I want my prayer to be that I might be consumed. *Oh Lord, make me kindling. At every change You bring into my life, may I respond in a way that shines glory right back to You. As You change me, I rejoice that You never change. May I be consumed by Your glory so that all that's left is more of Your fire. Shine, Oh Lord, shine!*

Are you still struggling with change? Are you putting off changes you know the Lord has already called you to make? Are you continuing to wrestle against some He has already made in your life? Encounter the Light, the Fire, the Author, and Finisher of our faith. Eyes off self, eyes off the change, and eyes onto the Savior. As the refrain of that sweet hymn encourages us:

> Turn your eyes upon Jesus,
> Look full in His wonderful face,
> And the things of earth will grow strangely dim,
> In the light of His glory and grace.

("Turn Your Eyes Upon Jesus," by Helen H. Lemmel, 1922, public domain.)

Learning to shift gears gracefully, walking with Jesus in every season and through every change can become habit-forming in the sweetest way. Sweeter than the party-sized Butterfinger. And without the sparking thighs.

A LITTLE EXTRA LIGHT FOR THE PATH:

"Who among you fears the LORD and obeys his servant? If you are walking in darkness, without a ray of light, trust in the LORD and rely on your God."
—Isaiah 50:10 (NLT)

HOW MANY LIGHTBULBS CHANGE THEMSELVES?

13

"Blessed are those . . . who walk in the light of your presence, LORD. For you are their glory and strength" (Psalm 89:15, 17).

My computer told me I should erase my history. I chose the 80s—solely on the basis of hair. Thankfully my hairstyle changes on a biweekly basis. That way I can't be caught in the same embarrassing style for more than a couple of incriminating pictures in a row.

Every once in a while, I like to do a big-time hair change-up for the travel adventure alone. When I'm speaking somewhere and I'm picked up at an airport by people I've never met, I have to admit it's sort of fun to watch them holding a sign with my name for a few minutes before I confess I'm the one they're looking for. The people generally will look at some publicity photo they have of me, then they'll look at me. Pause. Look at the photo. Back at me. Pause. Then they'll move on to try to find someone who looks more like me than I do.

Yeah, like I would ever have a publicity photo that actually looks like me. It's not just the hair. All authors and speakers are required to have a publicity photo. But nowhere in any of the contracts is it written that the photo has to be an accurate representation.

PICTURE THIS

I'm telling you, I have a genuine sympathy for photographers. Authors want a photo that looks natural. We want it to depict who we really are. And yet we don't want any wrinkles. Or spots. Or multiple chins. Or those glasses. Or that nose. And those cheekbones have to go. And pretty much that entire face altogether. It's a total no-win for the photographer.

When publicity photo time arrives, I've now completely given up the pretense and resorted to a makeup job that essentially involves painting over everything on my face that I don't like. Can I pretend that looks natural? Then I still ask the photographer to do some major touch-up—starting with making it into a uni-chinned photo, thank you.

By the time we're both done, I'm Halle Berry. No one can find me at the airport, but boy do I take a mighty fine pic.

CERTAIN "DRAWBACKS"

Doing my makeup these days has become sort of a color-by-number project anyway. There are a few disadvantages for all of us who've gone that "erase the face, then redraw it in" route. For instance, I told one of the sweet little ladies at church she might be penciling in her eyebrows a little too high.

She looked surprised.

Relatedly, I've run into several women who have not fully embraced where their lips end. Not to be tacky, but it's like they never learned to color inside the lines. Those preschool years? Very important.

There are certain face projects that should probably not be left to do-it-yourselfers. Anytime you need to change the location of an immobile body part, I can't see how that's going to happen without professional help.

BACK TO THE DRAWING BOARD

Trying to change ourselves on the inside is even more futile. Let's back up and think it through again. We don't change ourselves in that initial work of salvation. Why would we ever think we could change ourselves in the process of our sanctification? It's time to call in The Professional. Jesus says in John 15:5, "Apart from me you can do nothing."

Paul got it. In Philippians 3:3 (NLT) he says, "We rely on what Christ Jesus has done for us. We put no confidence in human effort."

Society continually sends us the message that we need to have self-confidence. But self-confidence is not only wishy-washy and unreliable, it's ineffective. Want real change? Change self-confidence to God-confidence. It's never misplaced. A person surrendered to Christ and confidently relying on Him will be changed. Period.

The more we know about our God, the more confidence we have in Him. The more we comprehend even the tiniest bit about how powerful He is, the more confident we are that He will change us in every way we need to be changed.

GLIMPSES OF HIS POWER SHINING THROUGH

In Matthew 17 we're given the picture of the light of Christ on the Mount of Transfiguration. Some of His God power was allowed to shine through a little as Peter, James, and John looked on. "As the men watched, Jesus' appearance changed so that his face shone like the sun, and his clothes became as white as light" (Matthew 17:2 NLT).

Just a peek and it was almost more than Peter, James, and John could take. Moses and Elijah appeared with Jesus, and the voice of God from a cloud said, "This is my dearly loved Son, who brings me great joy. Listen to him" (v. 5 NLT). The disciples were so shaken by it all that they fell flat on their faces. What a scene it must have been! Jesus revealing His glory light and God giving the Son a glorious validating tribute.

Our mighty Father, God, our conquering Savior, Jesus, and our powerful, heart-changing Helper, the Holy Spirit. As those who've surrendered our lives to the Lord, we have Him living inside us. He's available, offering strength for every situation. He guides, He comforts, He empowers. Why would we pursue strength anywhere else? And why would we ever rely on ourselves?

Doing the right thing is just too difficult in our own strength. Ours won't cut it. Making right decisions is no better than a wild guess if we're depending on a fleshly mind. Still, some try it. They rely on their own strength and energy and on their own perceptions and reasonings. And you can easily guess where that leaves them. Powerless and pitiful. Without His strengthening power we have no victory.

Just as true, when we receive His strength by yielding to His indwelling Holy Spirit, there is power. Big power. We looked at Acts 1:8 (AMP) in chapter 3: "But you shall receive power (ability, efficiency, and might) when the Holy Spirit has come upon you." The Greek word for "power" in this verse is *dunamis*, from which we get our word *dynamite*. That means that we're not talking about small power here. This is radical, life-changing, explosive power!

POWER FOR THE IMPOSSIBLE

When we assume we can change ourselves without the Lord—or that we can do anything of true value without Him—we reveal prideful thinking. "We don't have the right to claim that we have done anything on our own. God gives us what it takes to do all that we do" (2 Corinthians 3:5 CEV).

Are you resting in His power? Or are there things in your life you've been trying to accomplish on your own? Are you making decisions according to the strength and truth of His thinking instead of your own? Could I encourage you to begin each day recognizing your need for His strength, confessing that need to Him, and depending on Him to enable you to live well in His light? When it comes to changes you'd like to see happen in your life, you simply can't lean too hard on Him. Ask Him for His strength, allow Him to work through you, and then just watch as the impossible happens!

And that, my friends, will really raise a few eyebrows!

A LITTLE EXTRA LIGHT FOR THE PATH:

"So we keep on praying for you, asking our God to enable you to live a life worthy of his call. May he give you the power to accomplish all the good things your faith prompts you to do. Then the name of our Lord Jesus will be honored because of the way you live, and you will be honored along with him. This is all made possible because of the grace of our God and Lord, Jesus Christ."
—2 Thessalonians 1:11–12 (NLT)

LIVING IN THE LIGHT/ DWELLING IN HIS PRESENCE

"May God be gracious to us and bless us and make his face shine on us—so that your ways may be known on earth, your salvation among all nations" (Psalm 67:1–2).

My wonderful hubby surprised me last year with an anniversary cruise. Hawaii, baby! We had the most marvelous time just being together for seven glorious days. It was perfectly wonderful in every way.

I admit it, I'm a cruise fan. I love everything about it—especially the food. A cruise and overeating go together like a hand in glove. Well, more accurately, they go together like a size 10 hand in a size 2 glove. It's all the gourmet food you can eat, for crying out loud. I guess I was just asking for a trip back to maternity pants. I now refer to myself as "17 years postpartum." The staff on the ship said that the average person gains seven to ten pounds on a seven-day cruise. But then, I've always considered myself an overachiever.

On prime rib night, we were walking out of the dining room and, even though he was about to let his belt out a notch, Richie said he was thinking of ordering yet another prime rib. Another one! I figured that could cost him at least another two belt notches. I told him I thought that would be a mistake. Get it? Prime rib? "Mis-steak"?

HOW WOULD YOU LIKE THAT DONE?

Anytime we're going to overdo, though, it's good to make sure we're "overdoing" in all the right areas. Exceeding calorie limits? Not such a great thing to consistently overdo. But 1 Thessalonians 4:1 talks about living right to please God, and then it says, "Now we ask you and urge you in the Lord Jesus to do this more and more." To do and to overdo. It's an encouragement to keep growing. Not so much growing in the "bring on the elastic waistbands" kind of growth. But growing in maturity—sanctification.

Paul says in verses 2–3 of that same chapter, "For you know what instructions we gave you by the authority of the Lord Jesus. It is God's will that you should be sanctified." The Amplified Bible calls that sanctification, "consecrated (separated and set apart for pure and holy living)."

We grow as we seek to stay in the light, dwelling in the presence of the Lord, making sure our lives are for Him and all about Him. Our growth is not an option. It's a command. Verses 7 and 8 in that same passage in 1 Thessalonians say, "For God did not call us to be impure, but to live a holy life. Therefore, anyone who rejects this instruction does not reject a human being but God, the very God who gives you his Holy Spirit."

It can be a little startling to think that to reject His instruction and the call to pursue a holy, consecrated life is to reject our heavenly Father Himself. And that rejection means we're ignoring the Holy Spirit He gave to help live that life. Mistake of the highest order.

Growing in Him and dwelling in His presence results in a life in which growing "a notch or two" spiritually is a regular occurrence— the good kind of growth—and one where we seek that consistency in growth more diligently than we would seek the biggest everything-fried-to-perfection buffet.

FRY. FRY AGAIN

It was probably the one food the cruise ship didn't offer, but a friend was telling me about going to a restaurant for…are you ready for this?…chicken-fried bacon. No kidding. I'm sorry, but I can't imagine looking at bacon and thinking, "OK, just in case there's not enough lard here, and just in case it's not quite unhealthy enough, let me add some more fat and fry this puppy again." Chicken-fried bacon! Maybe it would be better if they rolled it in Lipitor first. Who knows, it might make a nice batter. My triglycerides are getting dizzy just thinking about it. But really, couldn't the bacon fryers' slogan be: "Double your pleasure, double your heart disease"? Surely that's a dish that should come with a crash cart on the side.

It might surprise you that the prospect made me think of the privilege of prayer. There's a double pleasure to be found there. I simply can't overestimate the catalyst prayer is as an agent of change and as a key to living in the light and dwelling in the presence of the Lord. There is power in prayer, and I believe our prayers can even influence God's decisions. But doubled with that is the additional truth that prayer is not designed to force our heavenly Father to see things our way, to change His mind about what we want. Prayer is about helping us see things His way, to help us put on His mind.

Deuteronomy 4:29 (NKJV) says to "Seek the LORD your God, and you will find Him if you seek Him with all your heart and with all your soul." There is victory in the sanctifying walk in the light as we ask the Lord to help us make that heart-and-soul-seeking kind of prayer part of our every day.

HEART AND SOUL

Recently my kids told me that I was whistling the "Heart and Soul" song. I didn't even know I was doing it. Well evidently I'd whistled it for a while. And they told me I then whistled it another couple of whiles. I whistled it until everyone in the family was ready to bang each of their respective heads against the nearest piano keys. I thought it was pretty funny that I could make them all that crazy without even realizing I was doing it. One of these days I might learn to listen to myself.

Oh that I may come to the place where following the light of Christ comes so naturally that I hardly know I'm doing it. May it become the habit of my life. It requires allowing Him to work on my character, to change me, to grow me. It requires making sure that Christ is my life and that my heart's desire is to love and obey Him with every ounce of "heart and soul."

Bad habits seem to form so much more easily than good ones. Even now that I'm not on a cruise ship, for instance, I have to admit that overeating is still a temptation. It doesn't help that my refrigerator keeps pressuring me to eat at night. That's got to be what it's doing. Otherwise that light inside there would just be wasted.

I never want to waste the light, spiritually. I'm praying the Lord will make me hungry to become hungrier. Thirsty to become thirstier. *Oh Lord, light the way for "more and more."*

A LITTLE EXTRA LIGHT FOR THE PATH:

"Finally, brothers, we instructed you how to live in order to please God, as in fact you are living. Now we ask you and urge you in the Lord Jesus to do this more and more. For you know what instructions we gave you by the authority of the Lord Jesus. For God did not call us to be impure, but to live a holy life. We urge you, brothers, to do so more and more."
—1 Thessalonians 4:1–2, 7, 10

UNFORGIVENESS BRINGS DARKNESS

"The LORD's *light penetrates the human spirit, exposing every hidden motive"* (Proverbs 20:27 NLT).

I consider my fingernails ten little accessories for my hands. I have a rainbow of polishes so my nails can change with my outfit and my mood. Wouldn't it be handy (hand-y?) if someone actually made a "mood polish" that could change colors? Mood messages for friends and family. Bright, happy-colored nails? Good time to ask a favor. Mellow, gloomy-colored nails? Approach with caution. Black nails? Run away.

Sometimes I still ignore my polishes o' plenty and invest in the acrylics. Nothing like a French mani to make a girl feel a little posh and…well, almost French. There's a hitch in polishing my nails myself anyway. I'm an extremely right-handed person. That works out great for the nails on my left hand. But I wonder how often I've looked down at that right hand only to wonder if those nails had been painted by a trained badger—one that wasn't all that well-trained at that.

NAILING DOWN COMMITMENT

Each time I write a book, at the beginning of that point when a tingle of near-panic tells me I'm closer to the deadline than I think, there's a special ceremony that takes place. The big event is called The Grand

Clipping of the Nails Ceremony. It's not a formal attire event, but it is steeped in rich tradition. A pinch of pomp and plenty of circumstance. It symbolizes cutting away the things that might hinder reaching the deadline. And it symbolizes the sacrifice. Oh, the sacrifice. Off with the nails of the long and lovely variety. It's sort of my way of affirming that the message of the book is more important than looking adorable. Very moving, I know. I'm tearing up a little even now—looking down at my short nails (though I do admit they're hot pink).

So this is the hot pink charge to ever and always stay committed to cutting away whatever might hinder our ministries. We need to stay passionately committed to cutting away whatever might hinder any part of our walk in the light at all.

I spoke with a woman not long ago who was very aware of a dark shadow of unforgiveness obstructing her light-walk. Someone in her life had hurt her deeply, and she simply couldn't see past that hurt. She said the darkness seemed to be more smothering every day.

DON'T CHIP THE POLISH

All of us have hurts and offenses we're forced to deal with. Some are annoyances, dealing with people who are rude and spiteful. I have an acquaintance who often cops a 'tude, for instance. I'm not sure why she has that chip on her shoulder, but it always helps me when I picture it as a Dorito. Just saying. But there are other offenses that go much deeper than annoyances. Deep wounds or abuses that scar. We need to first understand that we can't chip away at either depth of offense on our own.

Those smaller annoyances? We can rise above those with patience through the power of the God of light. Colossians 3:13 (NLT) says, "You must make allowance for each other's faults and forgive the person who offends you. Remember, the Lord forgave you, so you must forgive others." We're instructed to forgive just as we've been forgiven— and that makes sense. And the deeper grievances? We're accountable to forgive those through His power as well.

NAILING IT DOWN

In Matthew 18, Peter asked Jesus how many times he should forgive when someone sinned against him. "Up to seven times?" (v. 21). I'm sure Peter thought he was showing some very spiritual, above-and-beyond-the-call generosity there. But Jesus answered him, "I tell you, not seven times, but seventy-seven times" (v. 22).

Christ nailed him, as it were. Then Jesus told a story about forgiveness. It was about a king who forgave the debt of a man who owed something near national debt level—more than the guy could repay in his entire lifetime. That same man turned right around and showed no mercy to another guy who owed him one of those measly-five-bucks kinds of debts. Though the debtor begged for forgiveness, the man refused to release him from the debt. When the story got back to the king, he was furious that one who had been forgiven such a huge debt was unwilling to forgive even a small one. The king tossed the unforgiving man into prison and threw away the key.

We are that unforgiving man when we refuse to offer forgiveness. Though our sin debt was more than we could ever pay, Jesus offered His own life so that our debt could be forgiven. How can we ever refuse to forgive another's hurtful offense when we've been forgiven so much and so freely? Our forgiveness was purchased through the most important nails in all of history. No polish on these nails—only pain and shameful ruthlessness from those who drove them through the hands and feet of our Savior. And what was our Lord's incredible response to his persecutors even then? "Father, forgive them."

BITTERNESS JAILBIRDS

Bitterness becomes a prison for us as surely as it did for the unforgiving man in Jesus' parable. It traps us in time loops of rehearsing that person's offense over and over. It snares us in the bitter speeches we deliver to the offender in our minds. We're imprisoned in thoughts that wiggle out of our control, in fruitlessness, and even in a hindered prayer connection with the Father. Matthew 6:14–15 (*The Message*) says, "In prayer there is a connection between what God does and what you do. You can't get forgiveness from God, for instance, without also forgiving others. If you refuse to do your part, you cut yourself off from God's part."

Some withhold forgiveness because they feel to offer it would condone the sin of the offender. But forgiving doesn't mean we're saying what the person did was OK. It means we're choosing to let go. We're choosing not to hold on to that offense, letting go of pain and hate—and letting go of any nagging feeling that we need revenge.

Have you ever found yourself feeling you can't quite stay fixed on the course of light? You know you've given Christ your life, yet you can't seem to experience victory in your walk? Bitterness can do that. It casts a dark shadow on every aspect of life. Even when there's a victory, it's never as sweet. Bitterness affects how we treat our loved ones, how we see life—everything. Mood nails in every shade of black.

GOT A LIGHT?

When we forgive as we've been forgiven by the Father, the light switches right back on. That stifling darkness lifts, the smoke clears. We're free. It doesn't usually change the offender. It changes the forgiver.

The person I mentioned earlier who couldn't seem to get past the hurt someone had inflicted found her way out of her dark prison. She asked the Father to help her forgive. Some days she has to ask again and to forgive by faith, but she is experiencing new freedom in the light, and the dark times are coming fewer and farther between. It's often a choice we make day by day to say no to bitterness and to embrace the freedom of forgiveness.

Are you ready to say no to the darkness of bitterness and invite His light back into your life? You can pray something like this:

Heavenly Father, I've been walking in this dark place of unforgiveness far too long. Please forgive me. May today be the day I flick on the light—all by Your power and Your grace. I ask that You would grant me the strength to let go of that ugly grievance I've been allowing to darken my life. Father, I know it's Your will that I forgive. And I know You answer every prayer that's in Your will. So by faith and by the grace You give—and because of the forgiveness You have so freely given me—I forgive my offender.

Lord, if at any time I let the bitterness start to creep back in, I ask that You would convict me instantly to let it go again by Your strength. Thank You for your light. May I continue to walk in that light and live in the sweet freedom You give. Through Your power and in the name of the Savior, Jesus, amen.

PUT DOWN YOUR GRUDGE. PICK UP YOUR CROSS

Light waits for you at the end of that prayer—a bright light of blessed freedom. You may find yourself walking in new glorious places in the light, maybe even serving Him and pointing to His glory like never before as you're able to lay aside the heaviness of that bitterness burden and again pick up the Lord's call.

Keeping our guard up for any sneaky unforgiveness will most assuredly lead to life in a better light. Let's aim for staying in that Sonshine. That's exactly how to go to your happy-polish place.

A LITTLE EXTRA LIGHT FOR THE PATH:

"And do not grieve the Holy Spirit of God, with whom you were sealed for the day of redemption. Get rid of all bitterness, rage and anger, brawling and slander, along with every form of malice. Be kind and compassionate to one another, forgiving each other, just as in Christ God forgave you."
—Ephesians 4:30–32

PART 4

WATT IN THE WORLD?

—LIVING IN THE LIGHT GLORIOUSLY SPILLS OVER

LIGHT-LIVING TESTIFIES OF OUR ALL-SUFFICIENT GOD

"*Both day and night belong to you; you made the starlight and the sun*" (Psalm 74:16 NLT).

There's hardly anything I enjoy more than a good meal. That's probably why I don't cook much.

I guess that's also why I love, love, love whoever it was who invented the marvelous, miraculous…frozen dinner. What a genius! I owe this person. Everyone talks about those fancy ice sculptures. But to me? A frozen family-sized lasagna—now there's a thing of beauty. A centerpiece you can sink your teeth into!

Those frozen masterpieces not only rescue those of us who are oven-challenged, but they're also great for helping with that "what to have for dinner" decision. Anytime I've stared blankly into the pantry for more than a few minutes and still can't decide, I head straight for the freezer. I open that magic door and find, oh glorious day, someone has already decided! Other times when I'm having a bad grocery day and there aren't enough ingredients in there to put together anything besides a pickle-loaf/refried bean/Pringles casserole, I check that freezer—and dinner is done! Some days I just plain don't want to spend an hour in the kitchen. Sort of reminds me of my most convicting lightbulb joke: How many hormonal women does it take to change a lightbulb? ONE! Wanna make somethin' of it?!

The frozen dinners aren't bothered by the emotional upheavals. Having a bad estrogen day? No problem. In the freezer, dinner is already done! If they made it any easier they would be digesting it for me.

I'm embarrassed to admit how much I depend on my freezer for dinner (though, for the record, I do try to make sure I do all my own digesting). And working in exquisite harmony with my freezer, I can't forget my microwave. My beautiful, beautiful microwave. We've never needed a dinner bell. The beep of the microwave signals everyone that dinner is ready. That beep has become music to my ears.

THE PERFECT CENTERPIECE

Even sweeter music to my ears? A testifying song of an all-sufficient God. "For you make me glad by your deeds, Lord; I sing for joy at what your hands have done. How great are your works, Lord, how profound your thoughts!" (Psalm 92:4–5). Eternally sweeter!

It would be difficult to stand in the light of all He has done and keep that joy song inside. His works truly are amazing. We can center our lives on our all-sufficient God and His amazing provision. To think that His thoughts were toward us even before creation is mind-boggling. Our salvation? From the beginning of time, sound the glorious beep, it was planned and done!

We underestimate His greatness all too often. Our finite minds are stretched to the max trying to wrap themselves around His immenseness. I continue to be fascinated that He chose to manifest Himself to us through light in so many instances. From the very first day of creation, item one on His list of creations was light. Do you find it as intriguing as I do that though light had already been created, He didn't create the sun, moon, and stars until the fourth day? We think of the sun as the source of light, but it came later. God is the source of that light. He is more gloriously complex than we can fathom. He created the sun as more of a "place holder" for His glory. The God of light is the God of life itself.

DELIGHTING IN HIS SUFFICIENCY

There is comfort, delight—even celebration—in recognizing His all-sufficiency.

"How precious is your unfailing love, O God! All humanity finds shelter in the shadow of your wings. You feed them from the abundance of your own house, For you are the fountain of life, the light by which we see" (Psalm 36:7–9 NLT).

All that is good, every provision in this world, has its source in the God of light. James 1:17 (ESV) tells us that "Every good gift and every perfect gift is from above, coming down from the Father of lights." In the Greek, the "good gift" and the "perfect gift" are actually two different gifts. Two distinctive words are used for the gifts. The first emphasizes the graciousness with which the gift is given. The second focuses on the gift itself and its complete sufficiency. The "Father of lights," who power-spoke the sun, moon, and stars into existence, is the gracious source of it all.

In chapter 2 we looked at John 8:12 where Jesus declared that He is the Light of the world. He backed this up in the next chapter with a miraculous demonstration of His light power. He again said, "I am the light of the world" (John 9:5), and then He spit on the ground, made some mud, and put the mud on the eyes of a man who had been blind from birth. Jesus told the man to go and wash in the Pool of Siloam and when he did, oh, miracle of miracles, the man could see! This man had never seen light, never known anything but darkness all his life. Yet with dirt and spit, Jesus washed away the darkness. For the first time in his life, he could see!

WHAT HAPPENS WHEN WE SEE?

Our all-sufficient Lord provides for us in our blindness still today. Spiritual darkness was once all we knew—we weren't able to see the glory of God. But when Christ came into our lives, He washed away the darkness that held us captive, and we can now see to walk in His light. At the beginning of His ministry, He stood in the synagogue and read:

> "The Spirit of the Lord is on me, because he has anointed me to proclaim good news to the poor. He has sent me to proclaim freedom for the prisoners and recovery of sight for the blind, to

set the oppressed free, to proclaim the year of the Lord's favor"
(Luke 4:18–19).

Then Jesus told them, "Today this scripture is fulfilled in your
hearing" (v. 21).

What happens when we encounter an all-sufficient God? We're
changed! We no longer desire those dark places. We can see to walk in
the light! We're able to recognize the gifts from the Father of lights. As
we recognize His all-sufficiency, we're inspired and motivated to serve.
We're able to love with His kind of love. He gives us the desire and
the ability to shine His blessings back to others. He opens doors of
opportunity for us to shine in His service. He created the sun to be a
placeholder for His glory. He created us to be glory placeholders too.

LIGHTING UP THE OPEN DOORS

No matter what's for dinner, let's keep on making Him the centerpiece
of our lives, walking in His light and watching as He opens doors of
ministry and shows the way for us to shine.

Oh and just so you won't think I can't make a dinner without
opening the freezer door, we're having Italian tonight. Nothing frozen.
Mostly because my special Italian sauce is from a jar.

A LITTLE EXTRA LIGHT FOR THE PATH:

"When he came to the village of Nazareth, his boyhood home, he went as usual to the synagogue on the Sabbath and stood up to read the Scriptures. The scroll of Isaiah the prophet was handed to him. He unrolled the scroll and found the place where this was written: 'The Spirit of the LORD is upon me, for he has anointed me to bring Good News to the poor. He has sent me to proclaim that captives will be released, that the blind will see, that the oppressed will be set free, and that the time of the LORD's favor has come.' He rolled up the scroll, handed it back to the attendant, and sat down. All eyes in the synagogue looked at him intently. Then he began to speak to them. 'The Scripture you've just heard has been fulfilled this very day!'"
—Luke 4:16–21 (NLT)

LIGHT-LIVING CHASES AWAY OUR FEARS

"The LORD *is my light and my salvation—whom shall I fear?"* (Psalm 27:1).

I don't care what anyone says, I never laugh in the face of danger. But sometimes, when danger isn't looking, I point and make faces and call it a big stupidhead. Of course, then if danger looks over, I look down and pretend I've been picking lint off my jacket the whole time.

I decided early in life it might be wise to give a respectable deference to danger and fear, at least to their faces. I guess it's partly because when I was a kid, Bozo the Clown used to sit in a dark corner of my room every night and brood creepishly. It was always in the same corner. Then in the morning he'd be gone and there would be a floor lamp there instead. Eerie.

Since I obviously know my way around the fear topic, here's my helpful tip of the day: If you're panicking, try taking deep breaths—unless you're panicking because you're drowning. Because then you're definitely going to need a whole different tack.

DEEP BREATHING EXERCISES

On the more serious side, though, isn't it glorious that as we breathe in the presence of the God of light, we see our fears fade? When the angel came to the shepherds to announce the birth of the Messiah, the glory-light must've been shocking. "The glory of the Lord shone around them, and they were greatly afraid" (Luke 2:9 NKJV). But the angel's first words to the shepherds were, "Do not be afraid" (v. 10 NKJV). No need to fear! In fact, the angel brought the good news that the birth of the Messiah was ushering in our salvation. Has there ever been a greater reason for rejoicing? And that's just what happened. "And suddenly there was with the angel a multitude of the heavenly host praising God and saying: 'Glory to God in the highest, And on earth peace, goodwill toward men!'" (vv. 13–14 NKJV). What a sound and light show that must've been! But the shepherds didn't stay frozen in fear. No, they got up and hurried off to find the Christ.

That angel chorus wasn't the only Jesus-welcoming light party. When the wise men sought the Messiah, they were led by God's magnificent starlight.

> "And there it was—the star they had seen in the east! It led them until it came and stopped above the place where the child was. When they saw the star, they were overjoyed beyond measure. Entering the house, they saw the child with Mary His mother, and falling to their knees, they worshipped Him" (Matthew 2:9–11 HCSB).

Light can lead us to that place of worship. Worship is the exhale as we breathe in His light.

Ever scared of the dark? When we get those dark fears out of the way, we're free to worship and praise—the perfect response as we encounter the Lord of light.

FEAR POWER

Fear can be devastatingly powerful. It can rear its ugly head at the most inopportune moments. And when it arrives, it all but takes over our thoughts. It's tough to think of anything else when fear makes its way into our gray matter.

In Psalm 27:1 (HCSB), David reminds himself of the God who chases away fear: "The LORD is my light and my salvation—whom should I fear? The LORD is the stronghold of my life—of whom should I be afraid?" Fear may be powerful, but it's nothing compared to our God.

Bozo? You got nuthin'.

When we think about the fact that God manifests Himself in light and then contemplate all light does, we can't help but see our courage bolstered, just as David did. Light shows the way, causes growth, provides safety from danger, and more. God is our light, our salvation, our safe place—a place of no fear. Anytime we're afraid of shadows in the night, we have the comfort of knowing we can flick on the light. "You, LORD, are my lamp; the LORD lights up my darkness" (2 Samuel 22:29 NLT). He is our nightlight—any time of the night or day.

Every time we think about His sovereignty and His power, we turn on the lights. We realize we have nothing to fear. Nothing will come into our lives that He can't handle.

NO HEAD-ROOM

When fear fills our hearts and minds, there's essentially no room for anything else. If we let fear rule us, it can become a way of life. It's like standing beside the lamp but choosing to stay in the darkness.

Have you let fear prevent you from doing some things you know the Lord has called you to do? Have you let it paralyze you? Fear is the opposite of trust. And we have a God who is completely trustworthy. His record is clear. He keeps every promise. If you allow it to, faith will conquer your fear.

Think of the things that cause you fear and stress. Is there anything you've come up with that's too big for God to handle? Anything that's too tough for Him? A health issue? He knit your body together. Financial stresses? He owns everything. A schedule out of control? He holds time in His hands. Family members or friends in trouble? He knows them inside out. Whatever the challenge, the Father loves you, and He desires to shoulder the burden for you. "Cast all your anxiety on him because he cares for you" (1 Peter 5:7).

THE COURAGE TO SHINE

How often do we allow fear to squelch the light we're called to shine into the world? That fear isn't from the Lord. Paul tells us in

2 Timothy 1:7–10 (ESV):

> "For God gave us a spirit not of fear but of power and love and self-control. Therefore do not be ashamed of the testimony about our Lord, nor of me his prisoner, but share in suffering for the gospel by the power of God, who saved us and called us to a holy calling, not because of our works but because of his own purpose and grace, which he gave us in Christ Jesus before the ages began, and which now has been manifested through the appearing of our Savior Christ Jesus, who abolished death and brought life and immortality to light through the gospel."

Even Timothy needed to be reminded by Paul to dwell on the power and calling of God and to not let fear rule. The Father will give strength and courage to do what He calls you to do too. Breathe in His strength. Let it wash over your fears. Take courage and be a light in the world!

CAST AWAY

OK, ready to cast them? Cast all those fears 1 Peter 5:7 style into His capable hands. Give Him your list of worries. Once you've tossed them onto His strong shoulders, those anxieties are no longer yours. You don't have to drown in them a second longer.

That sets you free to worship Him and to serve Him. Are you passionate about sharing Christ's light in this dark world or have you been letting fear stand in your way? The Great Commission in Matthew 28:19–20 is your mission too. What's the worst that could happen if you boldly shared your faith? Can your God get you through that? Toss over the fear and let Him accomplish in your life what He desires to do through you.

Our calling to share is such a privilege. He chooses to allow us to be involved as a blessing. We don't share Christ to earn extra points with God. We come to Him in love and obedience and watch as He helps us overcome fear, putting in our hearts an urgency and a thrill in sharing Christ. Sharing the good news, the light of the gospel, becomes our delight!

Delight, my friends, in living in the no-fear zone—even if it never does become a no-clown zone.

A LITTLE EXTRA LIGHT FOR THE PATH:

"I take joy in doing your will, my God, for your instructions are written on my heart. I have told all your people about your justice. I have not been afraid to speak out, as you, O Lord, well know. I have not kept the good news of your justice hidden in my heart; I have talked about your faithfulness and saving power. I have told everyone in the great assembly of your unfailing love and faithfulness."

—Psalm 40:8–10 (NLT)

LIGHT-LIVING GIVES STRENGTH FOR EVERY CHALLENGE

"They did not gain victory with their own strength. It was your right hand, your arm, and the light of your presence [that did it]" (Psalm 44:3 GW).

My 17-year-old is the youngest of five kids. That means that poor Daniel has suffered a lot of wedgies through the years. But hey, I figure that'll give him stories he can tell his own kids someday. Some parents tell their children of the hardships of walking to and from school in the 12-foot snow, uphill both ways. My Daniel? He'll be able to tell his children that he spent several years suffering through underwear with no waistbands. Ah, the legacy. My friend Janet says he could call his life story "Wedgie Tales."

It's a good reminder that tough situations, like waistbands, will come and go. The real question is, how will we respond? Will we allow those difficulties to defeat us or will we allow them to strengthen us and change us? Will we rest in our heavenly Father's presence, seeing life from His eternal perspective? Or will we try to squirm out of those difficulties and make it through them on our own, pouting, whining, sputtering, and blaming all along the way?

"IF A SQUASH CAN MAKE YOU SMILE"

When the hardships of life threaten to squash us, we can find our strength and joy in the Lord. Nehemiah 8:10 says, "Do not grieve, for the joy of the LORD is your strength."

Stories of strength and grace under pressure are so much more fun to pass on to our children. These stories will even answer a lot of their questions about living in the light and how we are to do it. The stories can set a pattern for them to follow. Now there's a legacy.

In the Amplified Bible Version of 2 Corinthians 4:16–17 we read:

> "Therefore we do not become discouraged (utterly spiritless, exhausted, and wearied out through fear). Though our outer man is [progressively] decaying and wasting away, yet our inner self is being [progressively] renewed day after day. For our light, momentary affliction (this slight distress of the passing hour) is ever more and more abundantly preparing and producing and achieving for us an everlasting weight of glory [beyond all measure, excessively surpassing all comparisons and all calculations, a vast and transcendent glory and blessedness never to cease]!"

WASTING AWAY? NOT!

Waistbands? They're here today, wedgied away tomorrow. But we're to be focused on the eternal—the unseen blessedness that never ceases. Where there is glory! Where there is strength! Verse 18 says,

> "Since we consider and look not to the things that are seen but to the things that are unseen; for the things that are visible are temporal (brief and fleeting) but the things that are invisible are deathless and everlasting" (2 Corinthians 4:18 AMP).

I'm fighting the urge to mention that it says the visible things are "brief." Yeah, I'm totally leaving that one alone. But those invisible things? According to this passage, they're everlasting! Maybe not ever-elastic. But everlasting and completely deathless, for sure. And ultimately, in our own personal "everlasting," every question in this life, every why we've ever asked, will be answered in the most satisfying, resounding eternal amen of an answer.

The God of light provides strength for any and every challenge. Waste away? Never! We are strengthened by and through His grace. Paul understood those squashing situations:

> "A thorn in the flesh was given to me, a messenger of Satan to buffet me, lest I be exalted above measure. Concerning this thing I pleaded with the Lord three times that it might depart from me. And He said to me, 'My grace is sufficient for you, for My strength is made perfect in weakness.' Therefore most gladly I will rather boast in my infirmities, that the power of Christ may rest upon me. Therefore I take pleasure in infirmities, in reproaches, in needs, in persecutions, in distresses, for Christ's sake. For when I am weak, then I am strong" (2 Corinthians 12:7–10 NKJV).

We don't know what Paul's "thorn" was. We don't really need to know. All we need to know is that the grace of God was sufficient. And in that sufficient grace, Paul's weakness became his strength.

THE ANSWER FOR EVERY PRICKLY THORN

What is your thorn? Have you ever caught yourself thinking that your thorn is too big, too sharp, too…anything…for God? What or who else in all the universe is sufficient? Would you believe, not even the removal of that thorn would be sufficient for successful, satisfied, walk-in-His-light living? Only His strength-giving grace. His grace is deeper, bigger, wider, greater than even the removal of that trial in your life. "I am able to do all things through Him who strengthens me" (Philippians 4:13 HCSB).

If you're running out of juice, just plain exhausted as a result of dealing with difficult situations and difficult people, draw upon the strength of the Lord. Remember that He often uses those troubling circumstances and people to build character, to refine us. He actually uses them to bless us. If we attempt to handle it all in our own strength instead of relying on His, we completely miss the blessing. One of the most amazing things to see as we're walking in the light is the Father's changing work, transforming our weakness into His strength. "My power works best in your weakness" (2 Corinthians 12:9 NLT).

He provides strength for every weak place if you will fully rely on Him. "He gives strength to those who are tired and more power to those who are weak" (Isaiah 40: 29 NCV).

The grace of God is truly all you need. In dark times, let His grace light your way and become your light-living muscle. In His strength, your future is oh-so bright.

Pondering our bright future gives us an entirely different perspective on the momentary suffering. Even though in the present there still may be questions left temporarily hanging, strength for living and strength for trusting is available for the asking.

Incidentally, on the lighter side of those unanswered questions, this one still remains: Would you call a person living without waistbands a "wedge-etarian"?

A LITTLE EXTRA LIGHT FOR THE PATH:

"That's why, when I heard of the solid trust you have in the Master Jesus and your outpouring of love to all the followers of Jesus, I couldn't stop thanking God for you—every time I prayed, I'd think of you and give thanks. But I do more than thank. I ask— ask the God of our Master, Jesus Christ, the God of glory—to make you intelligent and discerning in knowing him personally, your eyes focused and clear, so that you can see exactly what it is he is calling you to do, grasp the immensity of this glorious way of life he has for his followers, oh, the utter extravagance of his work in us who trust him—endless energy, boundless strength!"

—Ephesians 1:15–19 (*The Message*)

LIGHT-LIVING SHINES JOY IN EVERY CIRCUMSTANCE

"Light shines on the righteous and joy on the upright in heart" (Psalm 97:11).

When you're having one of those vexing days when everything is bugging you, you really have to learn to take some of those bothersome annoyances with a grain of salt. Maybe several grains of salt. With chips under them. And also some cheese dip. Next thing you know, you're having your own little nacho party saying to yourself, "Hey wait, wasn't I bugged about something?"

I was on the hunt for a long-missing earring not too long ago and decided to look through several of my old purses. Vexing. But an adventure, nonetheless. It's amazing what you can find in an old purse that you don't remember ever having. A lone earring (though not the one I was looking for—argh), several pens advertising places I'd never heard of, plus—and this was not a great bonus, gotta say—there was a little river of spilled lotion down one side of the lining. I say lotion, but it was more congealed than lotion ever should be—more chewing gum than lotion. Unless it really was chewing gum. There was some of that in there too. I also found a giant lint ball that I initially mistook for a muskrat. Creepy. And may I go ahead and offer a little purse-search counsel here? If something is molding in there, just walk away. No earring is worth that.

OVER THE RIVER AND THROUGH THE PURSE

The only thing that kept me going was that I found a little bite-sized Almond Joy. You have to realize, I don't think I'd used this purse since 2004. But I still ate the candy. I think you know my policy on that by now. Hey, it was chocolate.

Did I mention the ton of Sweet'N Low packets I also found in there? That would've been a pretty nice find, except that some of them had leaked everywhere. White powder all over the inside of the purse. It looked like a drug bust gone bad.

When it comes to walking in the light, though, there really is no substitute. To miss the light is to miss the delight of real joy. There is joy in not settling for anything else but walking in His light, His way, His glory. Isaiah 61:10 says, "I delight greatly in the LORD; my soul rejoices in my God. For he has clothed me with garments of salvation and arrayed me in a robe of righteousness."

STEP INTO DE-LIGHT

To "delight" is to find satisfaction and pleasure. To "delight greatly in the LORD" is to find satisfaction and pleasure in Him alone, to have the kind of relationship with Him in which you find sweetest pleasure in spending time with Him. How amazing it is when we find that He desires that kind of relationship with us!

We develop that relationship by spending time with Him studying His Word and coming to Him in prayer and, as we trust Him, with every part of our lives. What joy there is in finding that through sweet fellowship, He's changing us. He's matching our hearts to His. Psalm 37:4 says to "Take delight in the LORD, and he will give you the desires of your heart." There's such joy in seeing our desires line up with His. Yes, great pleasure, delight, JOY, in walking hand in hand in the light with the God who loves us. Nachos can't begin to measure up. Not even a nacho party.

Joy is not giggly, silly giddiness. It's not even simply happiness. Joy runs deep. The Book of Philippians has long been my favorite book of the Bible because it's so full of overflowing joy. Yet Paul wrote the Book of Philippians from prison, chained to a Roman guard. Not a silly-giggly kind of happy situation, for sure. But Paul knew great joy. "Rejoice in the Lord always. I will say it again: Rejoice!" (Philippians 4:4).

THE WALK IN THE LIGHT IS A WALK OF FAITH

Walking in joy in the light isn't about merely waiting for the dark times to pass. Sometimes it's about learning to smile in the dark. It's about being assured that the light is there, even if you can't see it at the moment. It's about following hard. "My whole being follows hard after You and clings closely to You" (Psalm 63:8 AMP).

When times are dark, we're called to see life with eyes of faith. "Let us draw near to God with a sincere heart in full assurance of faith" (Hebrews 10:22). Even when difficulties hit, we can hang on to our joy as we understand that trials here don't affect our eternity. We've been adopted by our heavenly Father. We're His children. Romans 8:14–18 (NLT) says:

> "For all who are led by the Spirit of God are children of God. So you have not received a spirit that makes you fearful slaves. Instead, you received God's Spirit when he adopted you as his own children. Now we call him, 'Abba, Father.' For his Spirit joins with our spirit to affirm that we are God's children. And since we are his children, we are his heirs. In fact, together with Christ we are heirs of God's glory. But if we are to share his glory, we must also share his suffering. Yet what we suffer now is nothing compared to the glory he will reveal to us later."

Ours is a forever adoption.

As we know the Father's love, it changes how we look at life. It changes how we see difficulties and how we make our way through them. There's a vision change. "For we walk by faith, not by sight" (2 Corinthians 5:7 NKJV). Walking in the light, embracing the changes He makes in our hearts, allows us to see life through joy, no matter what our situation. "You've got my feet on the life-path, with your face shining sun-joy all around" (Acts 2:28 *The Message*).

His sun-joy? There's just no substitute. As for the sugar substitute, I'm not sure I want to go there anymore either. I think I've about decided to "just say no" to Sweet'N Low.

A LITTLE EXTRA LIGHT FOR THE PATH:

"Let those who love the LORD hate evil, for he guards the lives of his faithful ones and delivers them from the hand of the wicked. Light shines on the righteous and joy on the upright in heart. Rejoice in the LORD, you who are righteous, and praise his holy name."

—Psalm 97:10–12

LIGHT-LIVING INFUSES LIFE WITH HOPE

"For You cause my lamp to be lighted and to shine; the Lord my God illumines my darkness" (Psalm 18:28 AMP).

I was waiting for my luggage at the airport not long ago, and I made an interesting observation: I think about 90 percent of travelers have black luggage. If you have a black suitcase on wheels, forget about just reaching out, grabbing it off the belt, and rolling on your way. Just try it and you could very possibly get mugged by a dozen or so other black-luggage-lugging passengers. I had to take my husband's black luggage on a trip one time, and I lost two nails in a bad black suitcase scene. I think I still have a couple of emotional scars from that one. Talk about emotional baggage.

It was actually pretty funny what I saw at the airport this week. Tons of luggage was sliding down to the carousel, and every time the crowd spotted a black, wheeled bag coming down the pike, the entire mob leaned in as one. It was a little freaky. As the bag got closer, they would all circle around it like oversized vultures.

Three or four would reach for it to try to check the tags. Then there were several awkward smiles. And then for that one person (who had probably already reached for the wrong bag a good dozen times), it would be sort of like when you guess the right price from contestants' row and get to go up on stage with Drew Carey. Ding, ding, ding! "I won! It's mine!"

This time I got to simply stand back and observe. Why? Because my luggage is green. Not just green, but green with flowers. And if that's not distinctive enough, I've tied a white scarf in a giant bow around the handle. I can identify my luggage before it's even all the way down the chute. Never a doubt. I always know when mine is coming.

IT'S IN THE BAG

Jesus knows us that way. He can see us coming. It fills our lives with hope when we're assured that we are identified as His. And not only are we His, but He is ours.

The Bible tells us that everyone who is born of God wins. First John 5:4 says, "For everyone born of God overcomes the world. This is the victory that has overcome the world, even our faith."

Even more dark stuff is in this world than there is dark luggage. But for those of us who've by faith given our lives to Christ, a bright and shining hope is our ultimate victory. It's brighter than the brightest green luggage and more distinctive than any white bow. You can say, "I won! Victory is mine! Joy is mine! Jesus is mine!" "Let your unfailing love surround us, Lord, for our hope is in you alone" (Psalm 33:22 NLT). Hope is instant once we understand what it is to become—that green-flowered bag in a black-suitcase world.

HOPE ON A ROPE

Anytime you see yourself running a little low in the hope department, once again, check your quiet time. Been spending time in God's Word? Romans 15:4 (NCV) says, "The Scriptures give us patience and encouragement so that we can have hope." Hope! The Bible is our lifeline. Staying plugged in to God's Word is staying roped in to hope—and the patience and encouragement that help us get there. We're ushered into His presence, reading and studying His heart. And He meets us there. He meets our needs there. He infuses us with joy and hope at that sweet place.

Later in the same passage in Romans 15 (NCV), Paul writes, "I pray that the God who gives hope will fill you with much joy and peace while you trust in him. Then your hope will overflow by the power of the Holy Spirit." Hope that overflows! The importance of time with Him can't be overemphasized. No time with Him equals no hope. But the more we know Him, the more we're filled with untouchable hope—filled to overflowing.

The hope we're talking about here is not a "hope so" kind of hope. It's a sure hope. It's a "knowing"—the kind of knowing that changes the way you see your life and your future. Not a stab in the dark. A walk in the light.

HOPE CHANGES EVERYTHING

Mary Magdalene was no doubt heartbroken as she watched the brutal execution of the Lord she so loved. Jesus had changed her life in every good way. Yet at His death, she must've been thinking about how nothing would ever be the same. Everything had changed. He was gone. She came to the tomb "while it was still dark" (John 20:1). She came in darkness, not understanding. She left in light. She left understanding—"knowing"—that Jesus had risen. Before she left the scene at the tomb, the Lord appeared to her. Her heartbreak turned into rejoicing. Jesus had risen, and her life…had changed. Nothing would ever be the same. There was new, glorious hope.

Because Jesus is risen, He lives in us by His Spirit. That puts the hope on the inside. Colossians 1:27 refers to "Christ in you, the hope of glory."

Having that living hope on the inside emboldens us to share the same hope with others. Paul says in 2 Corinthians 3:12 (ESV), "Since we have such a hope, we are very bold." The hope of glory is not something we're to keep to ourselves. As a matter of fact, we're instructed to be ever-ready to share "Always be prepared to give an answer to everyone who asks you to give the reason for the hope that you have" (1 Peter 3:15). These verses were not directed specifically to the preachers and biblical scholars on some special missionary journey. No, they were written for the average traveler with bags in every size, shape, and color. They were written to you and me.

BAGS PACKED AND READY TO GO

So go ahead. Check the name tag. If you're His, your name is written in the Lamb's Book of Life. It's settled. Never a doubt. The suitcase is yours. It's a bag that comes packed full of all the hope you'll ever need to carry you joyfully through this life journey. And it means it's your calling to shine the hope in whatever corner of the world the Lord has placed you.

And this is actually one of those times when it's a good thing to be left holding the bag.

A LITTLE EXTRA LIGHT FOR THE PATH:

Therefore, since we have been justified by faith, we have peace with God through our Lord Jesus Christ. Through him we have also obtained access by faith into this grace in which we stand, and we rejoice in hope of the glory of God. More than that, we rejoice in our sufferings, knowing that suffering produces endurance, and endurance produces character, and character produces hope, and hope does not put us to shame, because God's love has been poured into our hearts through the Holy Spirit who has been given to us."

—Romans 5:1–5 (ESV)

PART 5

SANCTIFIED, ELECTRIFIED!

—LOOKING TO THE LIGHT

WORSHIP
IN THE LIGHT

"Praise the Lord, my soul. Lord my God, you are very great; you are clothed with splendor and majesty. The Lord wraps himself in light as with a garment" (Psalm 104:1–2).

I keep trying to find a friendly sounding alarm clock. Do you have one of those alarms that shrieks at the decibel level of a tornado siren? The alarm goes off, you jolt up in a panic, heart pounding, barely catching yourself before you sprint to the nearest storm shelter. Ever find those fingernail marks in the ceiling over your bed? And my alarm doesn't blast and then stop. It just keeps on shrieking. Smashing it with a fist does nothing—except cause major fist pain. Throwing it across the room doesn't faze it. Stomping on it doesn't do much either. Maybe you can guess why I never keep a sledgehammer beside my bed. Or a rocket launcher.

Why don't they make an alarm clock that gently jostles my shoulder while softly informing me that the cinnamon rolls are ready?

The thing is, if I ever found that kind of pleasant alarm clock, I'm pretty sure it wouldn't wake me. I guess there's purpose in the shriek.

A WAKE-UP TAZER

I'm convinced that there are times I need a soul alarm too. And not a soft jostle. A good jolt. In Psalm 57, David sounds the alarm with an "Awake, my soul!"

David says:

"My heart is steadfast, O God, my heart is steadfast; I will sing and make music. Awake, my soul! Awake, harp and lyre! I will awaken the dawn. I will praise you, O Lord, among the nations; I will sing of you among the peoples. For great is your love, reaching to the heavens; your faithfulness reaches to the skies. Be exalted, O God, above the heavens; let your glory be over all the earth" (vv. 7–11).

David is telling his sleepyhead soul to get in gear loving, serving, and glorifying the name of God. He's waking up that part of him that is built to praise and worship the God of the universe, readying himself for a new day of telling the whole world of the Father's wonderful love, of His amazing faithfulness, and of His vast glory.

Rejoicing in his circumstances? Not so much. David was in a cave, hiding from the king who hated him. He was in danger, running for his life. Sometimes when our circumstances aren't exactly the best, we need to awaken our souls to understand the goodness of God and to enthusiastically sing praises to the Father from every part of our being. David's dire circumstances and his unjust treatment screamed an urgency to share the Lord with a lost world, to contrast the wickedness of evildoers with the greatness of God. There was purpose in the shriek.

The Father's greatness always, always calls for celebration. Sometimes loud celebration. Sometimes quiet celebration. Me? Sometimes I might even wrap up the celebration with a cinnamon roll.

WAKE UP TO WORSHIP

It probably won't be a huge surprise to you when I admit what a worship wimp I can sometimes be. It's embarrassing. It's like I have spiritual ADD. I wonder why no matter what I'm doing, I'm thinking of the other things I should be doing. So often it even happens in my worship time. That special time becomes "interruptible."

Has it ever happened to you? You find you can't get through ten minutes of your Bible reading and prayertime without compulsively checking your email. Or you can't sit through an entire worship service at church without sneaking a peak at the newest incoming text message.

But our God is calling us to ignore the distractions, come aside, and…wait. Worship Him and wait. Our worship was never meant to be a time set aside for merely giving the Lord a to-do list or rattling off our own wants and feelings either. There's a place for our requests in our time with Him. But that's not the center of our worship.

In this day and age maybe more than any other in history, we continually feel the need to fill silence. If it gets too quiet, we reflexively flick on the TV or radio, check those Facebook notes or Tweets, or pop our cell phones in our pockets so we don't miss a text. It really can be alarming.

SILENT ALARM

There comes a time in every day when we need to pull the plug on all of it. We need to separate ourselves from every interruption and listen. Listen in the stillness, the quietness.

Remember that once you belong to Christ, the Spirit of God dwells in you. He has things He wants to communicate to you. Don't make those things difficult to hear. Don't let your life stay in noise mode so that His message can't get through to your heart. Even in your personal prayertime, could I encourage you to not let a silence be awkward? Let it be a special moment of worship when you welcome His presence into those sacred moments. Be comfortable in His presence. Invite Him to simply share the time with you.

ADHD is one thing. But the last thing I want is a spiritual deficit. There is no real spiritual muscle without the discipline and privilege of true worship.

TECHNO-MANIA

One of the reasons waiting quietly can be so challenging is that we do live in such a media-frenzied culture. We're constantly inundated with an incoming techno-signal of some kind or another. Email, phone calls, television, Facebook messages, radio, Tweets, mp3s, texts—and then, of course, more texts. My children are all in their teens and early 20s, and I honestly wonder if we would ever communicate at all if I didn't text. Our society is text crazy.

A friend of mine recently experienced a major texting disaster. Her thumbs were flying when with one bad thumb-move, she accidentally lost control and dropped her phone. That wouldn't have been so bad, except that the phone fell into a large container of water. I'm trying to keep it pleasant here, but let's just say that the next slogan for character-building week could be Just Say No to Toilet Texting.

I may have figured out why texting is so hot—and why it seems to happen nonstop these days. I think society is text manic because so many of us have decided we would rather talk—or type—than listen. Dishing it out, but not taking it, as it were. Tech-know-how lets us get across our own message, then skim the response. We can ignore the response altogether if we want. It's kind of the way of our society sometimes, isn't it? There's a blatant "me-centeredness" there.

NOW THAT'S ALARMING

The thought of that kind of selfish communion with our God is distressing, to say the least. He calls us to a different kind of connection. He says, "Be still, and know that I am God" (Psalm 46:10). He is God. He is the object of our worship.

Making our worship about our own personal needs and our own agenda is so profoundly silly anyway. Worship is focusing on Him. It's not about us and how eloquent or creative we can be. It's about how praiseworthy and how completely magnificent and how all-sufficient He is. It's not even about what you can do for your God in worship.

Moses participated in one of the most powerful personal worship experiences of all time. The God who is light appeared to him as a burning bush. "Moses saw that though the bush was on fire it did not burn up" (Exodus 3:2). God initiated the conversation by telling Moses that he was to remove his shoes because they were on holy ground. The presence of the Most Holy God made it a holy place and a holy moment.

The rest of their time together was all about what God would do. Even as Moses realized his own unworthiness and his own inability to make things happen in Egypt, the focus was brought right back around to the God who could empower him. "But Moses said to God, 'Who am I, that I should go to Pharaoh and bring the Israelites out of Egypt?' And God said, 'I will be with you'" (Exodus 3:11–12). True worship starts with recognizing the truth about who our mighty God really is. It's about praising Him for who He is and for His merciful provision of our Savior. It's bowing before that Savior, offering everything we are. It's communing with Him by His Holy Spirit.

John 4:23 (NLT) says, "But the time is coming—indeed it's here now—when true worshipers will worship the Father in spirit and in truth. The Father is looking for those who will worship him that way."

Let's commit to becoming more alert to worshiping in spirit and in truth. No pressing the snooze button.

Father, confirm in each of our hearts the urgency of connecting with You. As our souls start to get drowsy, Lord, I ask that You would awaken us to sweet worship times with You. Teach us to unplug and set aside every distraction. You are worthy of our undivided attention, our praise, our worship. Let us recognize Your holiness in those sweet, holy moments. May we worship You in spirit and truth, all glory light to You!

A LITTLE EXTRA LIGHT FOR THE PATH:

"One day Moses was taking care of Jethro's flock. (Jethro was the priest of Midian and also Moses' father-in-law.) When Moses led the flock to the west side of the desert, he came to Sinai, the mountain of God. There the angel of the LORD appeared to him in flames of fire coming out of a bush. Moses saw that the bush was on fire, but it was not burning up. So he said, 'I will go closer to this strange thing. How can a bush continue burning without burning up?' When the LORD saw Moses was coming to look at the bush, God called to him from the bush, 'Moses, Moses!' And Moses said, 'Here I am.'"

—Exodus 3:1–4 (NCV)

POWERING UP
FOR LIFE

"In a moment, in the twinkling of an eye, at the [sound of the] last trumpet call...we shall be changed (transformed)"
(1 Corinthians 15:52 AMP).

As I'm getting older, I notice my body parts are in a sort of snowballing landslide. I know the medical and cosmetic powers-that-be can work wonders these days with surgeries, injections, peels—tape this part up, snip that part off. I guess it's too bad I'm not desperate enough, brave enough, or rich enough to go any of those directions. Eventually I suppose I'll probably be looking for more necessary body repairs. A knee here, a hip there.

I wonder if they'll ever come up with a body parts game show. I can just imagine myself saying something like, "Alex, I'll take 'Prosthetic Joints' for $10,000." Or better, "I'll take the intestine to block."

Or better still, how about, "I'd like to buy a bowel, Pat."

BODY PART BINGO

One of the hottest topics on the Web, TV, magazines—every medium—is revving up the body to look better, feel better, function better. Some of the information is actually helpful. Other sources are playing an entirely different kind of game—a mind game. Need to lose some weight? They have hints, helps, and hype-up-your-metabolism pills. Need to exercise? Follow their plan and they'll make it "easy."

Want to feel great? Eat the latest life-saving miracle food "only available here!"

It's good to set goals to become better stewards of these bodies. We can be more fruitful if we're healthy. But it's also healthy to remember that focusing on the body—and its inevitable landslide—will leave us frustrated and sorely disappointed.

SLIP-SLIDING AWAY

So maybe it's also a good time to remember that this body isn't made to last forever. The good news? It doesn't have to. First Corinthians 15:51–52, 57–58 says:

> "Listen, I tell you a mystery: We will not all sleep, but we will all be changed—in a flash, in the twinkling of an eye, at the last trumpet. For the trumpet will sound, the dead will be raised imperishable, and we will be changed. But thanks be to God! He gives us the victory through our Lord Jesus Christ. Therefore, my dear brothers, stand firm. Let nothing move you. Always give yourselves fully to the work of the Lord, because you know that your labor in the Lord is not in vain."

Now there's an encouraging thought. Changed! In the most permanent, eternal way! We'll get bodies that no longer need medicines or surgeries. No nips, no tucks. No aches, no pains. No sorrow, no tears. A resurrected body designed by the Master Engineer to last for eternity.

Paul gives us some insight into our resurrected bodies in the verses right before in 1 Corinthians 15:42–44 (NLT:

> "It is the same way with the resurrection of the dead. Our earthly bodies are planted in the ground when we die, but they will be raised to live forever. Our bodies are buried in brokenness, but they will be raised in glory. They are buried in weakness, but they will be raised in strength. They are buried as natural human bodies, but they will be raised as spiritual bodies. For just as there are natural bodies, there are also spiritual bodies."

Good-bye, landslide. Hello, glorious new body! But the new body isn't even the best part. Trumpet, then *Jesus!* He's coming in the clouds to take us to be with Him. Slip-sliding away into an eternity with Jesus—and it's Jesus that will make heaven *heaven!*

CHANGING US THEN. CHANGING US NOW

How do thoughts of the ultimate eternal change in our future change us in the present? Those thoughts get us powered up for living in the light. Knowing Jesus could come any minute changes the way we think about these things:

*OUR PURSUIT OF PURITY AND OUR PERSEVERANCE—Watching for Jesus expectantly has a purifying effect on our lives. We're given a charge in 1 John 2:28 (AMP): "And now, little children, abide (live, remain permanently) in Him, so that when He is made visible, we may have and enjoy perfect confidence (boldness, assurance) and not be ashamed and shrink from Him at His coming." Caught in sin, red-faced when Jesus comes again—in the most embarrassing moment of all time? How sad that would be! In Matthew 24:36 Jesus tells us that no one knows the day or hour He'll return. Only the Father knows. Because Christ is coming again, and because He could come at any moment, we're inspired to steer away from sin and to stick to walking in His light.

*OUR PERCEPTION OF PLANTING AND OUR PROCLAMATION—Knowing the time until His coming is short changes the urgency we feel to share the message of redemption with those who don't know Christ. The thought of unbelievers suffering the punishment of an eternal hell compels us to plant the seeds of the gospel and to proclaim the good news with dogged zeal. Paul says in 2 Corinthians 5:18 (TLB), "God has given us the privilege of urging everyone to come into his favor and be reconciled to him." And in John 9:4 (NLT) Jesus Himself says, "All of us must quickly carry out the tasks assigned us by the one who sent me, because there is little time left before the night falls and all work comes to an end."

*Our Plans of Purpose and Our Passion—Anticipating Jesus' soon return excites us to serve. There's work to do while we're here, and knowing the Lord is coming soon ignites our passion to carry out our purpose. We don't want to let the time we have slip away fruitlessly. We looked at the instructions from Paul in 1 Corinthians 15:58 to "give yourselves fully to the work of the Lord" so that "your labor in the Lord is not in vain." *The Message* phrases it this way: "With all this going for us, my dear, dear friends, stand your ground. And don't hold back. Throw yourselves into the work of the Master, confident that nothing you do for him is a waste of time or effort."

CHANGELINGS

Focusing on the second coming of Christ can really change us. We're walking in the light as we're looking toward the eternal and not just the temporary here and now. Paul says in 2 Corinthians 4:18, "So we fix our eyes not on what is seen, but on what is unseen. For what is seen is temporary, but what is unseen is eternal."

A body that looks ready for Jesus' return definitely does not have to be one that has dodged the snowballing landslide with procedures or poultices. If we wait expectantly for Him, that's when we find ourselves walking in His light and looking truly mah-velous.

A Little Extra Light for the Path:

"For the Lord himself will come down from heaven, with a loud command, with the voice of the archangel and with the trumpet call of God, and the dead in Christ will rise first. After that, we who are still alive and are left will be caught up together with them in the clouds to meet the Lord in the air. And so we will be with the Lord forever. Therefore encourage one another with these words."

—1 Thessalonians 4:16–18

DEALING WITH THE DARKNESS

"If I say, 'Surely the darkness will hide me and the light become night around me,' even the darkness will not be dark to you; the night will shine like the day, for darkness is as light to you" (Psalm 139:11–12).

Have you ever had one of those mornings? I recently woke up to find that my coffeemaker had died. It seems it had passed peacefully during the night. A peaceful passing for the machine. Not such a peaceful morning for me. This girl likes her coffee.

To further complicate the morning, the Internet was down. Oh, the humanity—no email! So there I was, no Internet and no coffee. And also no axis for the world to spin upon. Earth had obviously slipped out of its orbit and rolled somewhere very dark.

I was grumbling about it all as I trudged across the family room when suddenly, mid-grumble, I realized I had stepped in a giant pile of cat barf. If that wasn't bad enough, something had obviously not settled well with the cat, and through the night my entire family room rug had been transformed into a barf minefield. If only I had realized that before I took the next step. You got it. Both feet. Oh. My. Gotta say, this was not settling well with me either. It was definitely not one of those picture-perfect moments.

Granted, people seem to have different ideas as to what constitutes a picture-perfect moment. I have a friend who hadn't looked through the pics on her digital camera for a few months. As she was scrolling through, she came across one that was especially interesting. She couldn't figure out what it was. Shades of chocolate brown and gray muted tones in a mix of textures, all surrounded by soft, smooth ivory colors. She studied it, analyzed it, changed it from vertical to landscape. Still, she couldn't tell what it was. She finally asked her teenage son. He said, "Oh yeah. The dog pooped on the kitchen floor, and I wanted you to know I cleaned it up." I guess it's OK she's not a scrapbooker. I shudder to think what themey stickers she'd be using for that page.

PICTURE THAT!

My dad once called me and asked me to start saving all my burned out lightbulbs. I asked him what he was going to use them for, and he said he was thinking of taking up photography and wanted to build a darkroom. Ah, my dad.

I've heard that if you hang out in a darkroom too long, you might not like what develops. Too many negatives.

Are you feeling like you've really stepped in it? There are seasons in life when those picture-perfect moments seem few and far between—time when your world rolls into a very dark place. Where is the God of light when you encounter the overwhelming darkness? Psalm 34:18 (NLT) reminds us that He is very near: "The Lord is close to the brokenhearted; he rescues those whose spirits are crushed."

Remember, in a world that still squirms under the curse of sin, bad things happen. When a crushing dark season comes your way and you're so overwhelmed by the pain that you can't see the light, rest in knowing that even in those times, the God of light is in control and He is close by.

THE BIG PICTURE

Never judge His love for you by your circumstances. Sometimes when the Father allows pain and tragedy to interrupt life, people may think He's not caring. How many times have you heard someone say that a loving God wouldn't allow us to suffer? His Word tells us that His ways are not our ways (Isaiah 55:9), and the truth is, we may never understand all the whys of suffering this side of heaven. But there's one thing you can always know. You can find sweet relief in this truth—that the love of God for you, His compassion toward you, and the grace He has for you are all bigger and brighter than the darkness you're experiencing. It's true. His love for you is immensely bigger than the pain you're suffering.

Nothing can interrupt His love for you.

"Can anything ever separate us from Christ's love? Does it mean he no longer loves us if we have trouble or calamity, or are persecuted, or hungry, or destitute, or in danger, or threatened with death? (As the Scriptures say, 'For your sake we are killed every day; we are being slaughtered like sheep.') No, despite all these things, overwhelming victory is ours through Christ, who loved us. And I am convinced that nothing can ever separate us from God's love. Neither death nor life, neither angels nor demons, neither our fears for today nor our worries about tomorrow—not even the powers of hell can separate us from God's love. No power in the sky above or in the earth below—indeed, nothing in all creation will ever be able to separate us from the love of God that is revealed in Christ Jesus our Lord" (Romans 8:35–39 NLT).

You can also know that in the big picture, He will make all things right. We won't live in a sin-cursed world forever. Our future holds everlasting triumph.

Psalm 40:1–3 reminds us of our imminent rescue from every dark place. "I waited patiently for the Lord; he turned to me and heard my cry. He lifted me out of the slimy pit, out of the mud and mire; he set my feet on a rock and gave me a firm place to stand. He put a new song in my mouth, a hymn of praise to our God. Many will see and fear and put their trust in the Lord." Mud, mire, or other family room rug atrocities, He will lift you. He will give you your footing back. And the result? A testimony of praise that will draw others to Him.

AVOID BUILDING YOUR OWN DARK ROOM

Through it all, the Lord wants you to experience His love in a close, personal way. When it's dark, don't let the enemy whisper in your ear that your God doesn't care. Believe that He is with you. Know that His grace will sustain you. In dark times, when you can't see the light, just touch the hands. Those hands are sort of monogrammed. The engraving has been done in your honor: "See, I have engraved you on the palms of my hands" (Isaiah 49:16).

If your struggle is with the darkness of depression, don't keep it to yourself or try to handle it on your own. Your Father is ready to be your lifeline. And He has placed godly friends, counselors, and physicians in this world He can use to help you.

Keep a tight rein on where you let your thoughts focus. Random thoughts will pop into your head, yes. But when those dark negatives creep in, you don't have to allow your brain to let them steep there. Scripture is a great antinegative. When dark thoughts threaten to crowd out the positive, get some thought renewal through His Word. Let it direct your thoughts God-ward in the direction of light.

> "Whatever is true, whatever is worthy of reverence and is honorable and seemly, whatever is just, whatever is pure, whatever is lovely and lovable, whatever is kind and winsome and gracious, if there is any virtue and excellence, if there is anything worthy of praise, think on and weigh and take account of these things [fix your minds on them]" (Philippians 4:8 AMP).

Keep in mind—and close to heart—that a dark season is just that. A season. Joy is around the corner for you. "Weeping may tarry for the night, but joy comes with the morning" (Psalm 30:5 ESV). Hang on. Morning is coming.

ON THE LIGHTER SIDE

There usually is a brighter side of every story—positives we can dwell on. We can choose to allow these brighter thoughts to lighten our load.

For instance, on the much lighter side, the morning I stepped in the steaming pile of cat barf with both feet? I'd borrowed socks from my daughter.

A LITTLE EXTRA LIGHT FOR THE PATH:

"My response is to get down on my knees before the Father, this magnificent Father who parcels out all heaven and earth. I ask him to strengthen you by his Spirit—not a brute strength but a glorious inner strength—that Christ will live in you as you open the door and invite him in. And I ask him that with both feet planted firmly on love, you'll be able to take in with all followers of Jesus the extravagant dimensions of Christ's love. Reach out and experience the breadth! Test its length! Plumb the depths! Rise to the heights! Live full lives, full in the fullness of God."
—Ephesians 3:14–19 (*The Message*)

LIMELIGHT VERSUS REAL LIGHT

"But everyone who lives by the truth will come to the light, because they want others to know that God is really the one doing what they do" (John 3:21 CEV).

I love the imaginative colors God uses when He puts His children together. But have you ever seen one of those fake orange tans? Honestly, I never judge a person by skin color—that's silly. Unless it's orange. And self-inflicted. Then, sorry, but I judge without mercy.

Don't get me wrong. I've done the tan-in-a-bottle thing plenty of times myself. But at the point I turn myself into an orangutan, I hope I have friends who love me enough to do an intervention. Or would that be more of a tannervention?

I actually tan much more easily these days than I used to. It's just that the tan comes in spots, and they're never where I want them. Still, I feel I look better in "random speckles of tan" than I do "age spots."

THE TANS THEY ARE A-CHANGIN'

If only the random color changes were the only problems I found myself "facing." I was looking through family pictures not long ago. I love oohing and aahing over the pictures of all my kids when they were babies. I did, however, make an interesting observation in several of the shots that included the entire family. When the kids were babies, my husband had a mustache.

And I didn't.

Whoa, not a pretty turn of events, I must say. I wonder if we could make a bad reality show out of it. Something like "Where's Their Hair Now"? Or even better, how about "Trading Faces"?

If not a reality show, at least a poem. I realize that after already giving you revealing examples of my poetry, mentioning another ode could cause you some major angst. Still, a traumatic event often calls for another round of bad poetry—maybe all the more if it involves facial hair. So brace yourself.

> Electrolysis or lasers?
> Should I go ahead and tweeze it?
> Sugars, waxes, creams, or razors?
> Should I heat it, blast it, freeze it?
>
> Maybe shaving, maybe bleaching.
> Gotta look at all the facts.
> I can simply wax poetic,
> But maybe I should simply wax.

I decided it was time to end the bad poem when I realized there were too many words that rhymed with "pelt" and not enough that rhymed with "weed-whacker."

A TALE OF TWO FACES

All *Extreme Makeover*, Face Editions, aside, if we want to shine the light of Christ, it's not a bad idea to stop and think about our spiritual faces. Have you ever met a two-faced person? Have you ever been one? Behaving one way at church, showing a totally different face at home, on the job, or at school?

We need to always put our best face forward, as it were. Hypocrisy is one of the Lord's pet peeves. We're told in 1 Peter 2:1 to stop all that nonsense. "Therefore, rid yourselves of all malice and all deceit, hypocrisy, envy, and slander of every kind." The New Living Translation phrases it like this, "So get rid of all malicious behavior and deceit. Don't just pretend to be good! Be done with hypocrisy and jealousy and backstabbing." Pretenders and two-faced back-stabbers? They need makeovers in the most extreme way. And on all their collective faces.

Jesus says in Mark 7:6, "Isaiah was right when he prophesied about you hypocrites; as it is written: 'These people honor me with their lips, but their hearts are far from me.'"

It doesn't even really matter who has the furriest upper lip. Whatever my lip condition, I never want it to be out of sync with my heart. I've given my heart to Christ. That means my lips are to be His too— all of me including all face places. Hypocritical behavior is a bust. And when we have secret places of hypocrisy in our lives, they interfere with our worship. After all, no secret places are hidden from Him. He sees our hearts. Isaiah 66:3 (AMP) says, "The acts of the hypocrite's worship are as abominable to God as if they were offered to idols."

LET'S FACE IT

Enough duplicity. We need to get rid of every two-faced tendency. I want to look forward to meeting Jesus face-to-face with great eagerness and expectation. Face-to-face. Not face-to-face-to-face.

I have to be honest. The Father has to constantly keep me in check in the hypocrisy department and in my tendency to be a spotlight-aholic. Both are pride issues. And both are sin. The message of this life is not about me. It's all about the God of light. And at the very point I can get my lime-lit self out of that spotlight, He is able to use me to shine the spotlight on Him— exactly where it should be.

John the Baptist got it.

"There came a man who was sent from God; his name was John. He came as a witness to testify concerning that light, so that through him all men might believe. He himself was not the light; he came only as a witness to the light. The true light that gives light to every man was coming into the world" (John 1:6–9).

John the Baptist's followers were upset that people who'd been following John were beginning to follow Christ. In John 3:30, John the

Baptist says, "He must become greater; I must become less." He tells his followers that the Father has placed everything in the hands of the Son.

TO BE A SON-LAMP

Jesus says of John the Baptist in John 5:35–36: "John was a lamp that burned and gave light, and you chose for a time to enjoy his light. I have a testimony weightier than that of John. For the very work that the Father has given me to finish, and which I am doing, testifies that the Father has sent me."

Jesus had our spiritual rescue to accomplish. Our eternal salvation had to be won. Jesus knew—and John knew—that the spotlight had to be on Christ and His redemptive work.

We need to keep the spotlight steady. The world is watching. And for many, their redemption is at stake. First Peter 2:11–12 (*The Message*) says:

> "Don't indulge your ego at the expense of your soul. Live an exemplary life among the natives so that your actions will refute their prejudices. Then they'll be won over to God's side and be there to join in the celebration when he arrives."

> *O Father, by Your grace, get my ego out of the way. Keep my pride in check. Forgive me when my life becomes more about me and what others may think of me than it is about You. Lord, let me bless and not simply impress. Please make me a lamp for You. Use me to reflect Your light, to shine so that others can see You. You must increase. I must decrease. Spotlight fully focused on You.*

Hypocrisy and pride? Anytime I'm in the spotlight or hogging limelight, it's time to change the spiritual bulb. It really is my heart's desire that I spend so much time in the Son-light that there's no room for anything fake. Here's hoping I can avoid everything "spiritually orange." Otherwise I have to judge myself without mercy.

A LITTLE EXTRA LIGHT FOR THE PATH:

"When swelling and pride come, then emptiness and shame come also, but with the humble (those who are lowly, who have been pruned or chiseled by trial, and renounce self) are skillful and godly Wisdom and soundness. The integrity of the upright shall guide them, but the willful contrariness and crookedness of the treacherous shall destroy them. They who are willfully contrary in heart are extremely disgusting and shamefully vile in the eyes of the Lord, but such as are blameless and wholehearted in their ways are His delight!"

—Proverbs 11:2–3, 20 (AMP)

HEADLIGHTS ON YOUR OWN DAMASCUS ROAD

"You, Lord, are my lamp; the Lord turns my darkness into light" (2 Samuel 22:29).

I like my car, but it's nothing fancy. No frills, no bells, no whistles. I do have seat warmers, but only on sunny days when the sun shines through the windshield just right. Still, maybe you'd be impressed to find out that my car's tank can go from $0 to $20 in, like, ten seconds flat.

I don't have the machinery, cameras, and various forms of car magic that will tell you you're about to bump something. I have to rely on my eyeballs and my rather bad spatial perception. That's probably why I feel I have to be one of those take-no-risks kind of drivers. Changing lanes for me is pretty dramatic. And I'm just warning you, it can be really annoying to get behind me on a two-lane highway. I hate to pass on those little roads, no matter how much good, clear road I have ahead of me.

The other day I was behind a slow-moving vehicle. It was one of those massive pieces of farm machinery on wheels with these machete-looking things poking out the side. No way was I passing that contraption. I had enough road ahead to land a small plane, and I still wouldn't go around. It didn't get embarrassing until someone passed my car and the machete-machine in one big go-round, and

I realized the vehicle passing us was carrying a prefab home. Seriously, how absurd is it to go so ridiculously slow that you get passed by a house?

CHANGING LANES

Paul had perhaps the most dramatic path change in all of history. His encounter with Christ is mentioned three times in the Book of Acts (Acts 9, 22, and 26). Before encountering the light of Christ on the Damascus road, he was called Saul of Tarsus, and most of his time and energy went to devising new ways to destroy Christians. He was heading to Damascus to round up some Christians and bring them back to Jerusalem as prisoners when God stopped him cold. "As he neared Damascus on his journey, suddenly a light from heaven flashed around him" (Acts 9:3). Paul described it as "a light from heaven, brighter than the sun" in Acts 26:13.

He fell on his face, and then he heard a voice saying, "Saul! Saul! Why do you persecute me?" (Acts 22:7). When he asked, "Who are you, Lord?" the answer was, "I am Jesus of Nazareth, whom you are persecuting" (v. 8). Paul got up from the ground a changed man. That showed up in his response, "What shall I do, Lord?"

ON THE ROAD AGAIN

Saul's plan had been to make a prideful triumphant entry into Jerusalem with Christian prisoners in tow. The light on the Damascus road had blinded him. He instead made his entry led by the hand like a little child. He was blind for three days until God called on Ananias to heal him. Wow, what a different road Saul of Tarsus took than what he had planned. What a change!

The change in him wasn't a temporary one. It was complete. He was transformed from one who fought Jesus at every turn and persecuted His people to one who ultimately endured suffering and terrible persecution himself for the cause of Christ. He surrendered his will to Jesus, and he was a new man. And God used him to change the church. Not only did Paul immediately preach Jesus boldly, but through it all, God used him to give us much of the New Testament.

We are charged to love and serve Christ just as Paul was. We're redeemed with purpose—to get in on what God is doing and to shine glory back to Him. It was Paul who was inspired by the Holy Spirit to write that we are to "shine as lights in the world" (Philippians 2:15 NKJV).

CHANGE OF HEART

The dramatic change of heart? It happened to Paul when he encountered the light. It happened to me as a little girl. I realized my sin and my need for a Savior and I gave Jesus my all. It happens to everyone who encounters the light and responds as Paul did, with repentance and with a "What shall I do, Lord?" And life is never the same.

Are you allowing Him to continue His changing work in you? Understand that when He changes your nature at salvation, that change is instant. Your direction immediately changes from hell to heaven. But the sanctifying change in you is a longer process. Don't doubt it. Know that He is at work. Trust Him.

STREET LIGHTS

Think again about some of the times God has chosen to reveal Himself through light. Not just any light. Spectacular, mind-blowing, eye-squinting, glorious light. The pillar of fire, the burning bush, Moses' face, the star that led to Bethlehem, the Mount of Transfiguration. At the end of the Book of Exodus when the tabernacle was finished, the light came down from heaven to dwell in the Holy of Holies. It was the light of the presence of God. Glory! Later when the temple was completed, again His glory light showed up to dwell in the temple. Shekinah glory!

Since the Holy Spirit now lives in us, we've become that place where His glory light dwells. He lights our way from the inside out—whatever street He may lead us down. According to Paul in Colossians 1:12–13 (NLT), the Father

> "Has enabled you to share the inheritance that belongs to God's holy people, who live in the light. For he has rescued us

from the one who rules in the kingdom of darkness, and he has brought us into the Kingdom of his dear Son."

Because we've been rescued, our future is bright. This world is not our home—prefab or otherwise. We get to spend eternity with Him. Jesus says in Luke 17:24, "For the Son of Man in his day will be like the lightning, which flashes and lights up the sky from one end to the other." We can look forward to the day when we're ushered into the glorious presence of our Lord in that place that will be lit by the glory of God with the Lamb as its lamp. And "the nations will walk by its light" (Revelation 21:24).

GLORY DOTS

When you glance at the sun, it's amazing how long you still see its dots even after you look away. As we look to the Son, let's let the glory dots last. Here's the charge to walk in the light: "For once you were full of darkness, but now you have light from the Lord. So live as people of light! For this light within you produces only what is good and right and true" (Ephesians 5:8–9 NLT). Illumination!

Let His Word light the way for how you're to live. Let His Spirit shine in your heart, revealing what needs to stay in your life and what should go. Let the Lord shine through you, lighting the dark places of the world. Be a bright spot for others by loving them into the light. In 1 Peter 2:9 (NLT) we see that we're God's chosen people and that we are to "show others the goodness of God, for he called you out of the darkness into his wonderful light."

O Glorious One, may we shine the truth of Your word, shine the light of Your love, shine the glory of Your salvation. May we shine Your wisdom, shine obedience and courage and joy, shine hope and blessings, shine to the world the glorious changes You make in us and through us. O Lord, let Your glory light shine! Let it change me. Let it change the world.

A LITTLE EXTRA LIGHT FOR THE PATH:

"You're here to be light, bringing out the God-colors in the world. God is not a secret to be kept. We're going public with this, as public as a city on a hill. If I make you light-bearers, you don't think I'm going to hide you under a bucket, do you? I'm putting you on a light stand. Now that I've put you there on a hilltop, on a light stand—shine! Keep open house; be generous with your lives. By opening up to others, you'll prompt people to open up with God, this generous Father in heaven."
—Matthew 5:14–16 (*The Message*)

DISCUSSION GUIDE

"In Light of All This . . ."

Would you like to see your life change right before your eyes? Do you long to have a life that pleases your heavenly Father? Do you long to understand just what it is that really does please Him?

If you're turning to this discussion guide for your own personal study time, that's wonderful. I think you'll find it adjusts well for adding a personal application or two in your light-seeking journey. Skip the "Get Glowin'" opener prompts and dive right into the questions for each chapter. There may be a few group-focused questions, but they're easily tweakable to fit your personal reflection time.

Shining the light group-style? Twinkle away! Here's hoping your light journey together will be illuminating in every good way.

DISCUSSION LEADER NOTES

Taking a group walk toward light-living? Brilliant! This light discussion guide should be just the ticket to give you hints and helps as you seek to apply some truths from God's Word. Reading a book can be enlightening. But how much more glorious it is when we set a higher goal than merely reading through material. That higher goal is to let it shine into our lives and allow the Holy Spirit of God to change us. To get personal—to truly take it to heart and see the difference following God's Word and its principles makes in our lives.

Watching the Spirit change your group right before your eyes, to the glory of God—it can happen!

The chapters can be divided up in whatever way best fits your group's needs and schedules. If you're up for a 13-week study, the introduction and chapter 1 would work well for the first week, then two chapters per week for 12 more weeks.

The questions in this guide are personal reflection questions designed to help us think about and fruitfully process what we've seen in God's Word. Each chapter will begin with a "Get Glowin'" discussion starter designed to help group members loosen up and hopefully generate a chuckle or two. Sometimes sharing on a surface level can break down barriers and free group members to later share on a deeper, more significant level. As the discussion leader, it's helpful if you have an answer or story ready for the discussion starter, just in case you might need to "open up the opener," so to speak. Shoot for hitting that balance somewhere between sharing enough of yourself on every level to allow your group to trust you, but not so much that you make the discussion too much about you. If you have a close friend or two in the group, it's a great idea to make yourself accountable to them and to ask them to honestly tell you if you're balancing well.

Be transparent. If you will be real—even if you have a struggle— your group will most often respect your genuineness, and they will feel freer to share their own struggles as they come up.

WHAT YOU'LL NEED TO DO EACH WEEK

Encourage your group to read the assigned chapter or chapters before the group meeting, but let them know that even if they get behind in reading, they still won't feel out of place coming to the discussion meetings. Reminders through phone calls or emails are great. You can divvy up those duties or ask one of your group members if they would consider being a contact person. Even with a contact person, as group leader, it's great to check in on your group whenever you can. Ask them how you may pray for them. Whether you contact them or not, may I encourage you to make a commitment to pray for each of your group members each week? What life-changing power there is in prayer!

As you're going through the week's assigned reading, make a few notes or observations you would like to point out or comment on during that week's discussion time. If the Lord teaches you something poignant, confronts you on an issue, or deeply moves you in some way, openly share that with your group.

After you've done assigned readings and prayed for your group, look over the discussion questions. Be ready to offer some answers if the discussion needs a little charge, but again, be careful not to monopolize the chat time.

GUIDELINES FOR DISCUSSION GROUP

You'll want to set up some ground rules for the group from the very first meeting. Here are some suggestions:

❑ Personal information shared within the group does not leave the group. Remind each other regularly that everyone should be able to freely share and know that no one in the group will ever betray a confidence.

❑ If someone shares a need or asks for prayer during a meeting, someone should volunteer right then to stop and pray for that need. Just a few sentences will be perfect.

❑ No cutting remarks or unkind comments to anyone in the group or about anyone outside the group. Uplifting, positive words only.

❑ Likewise, never correct anyone in front of the group. Belittling or embarrassing someone into changed behavior rarely works. If confrontation needs to happen it should happen in private and it should be done in love.

❑ If someone says something contrary to God's Word, however, let her know you respect her opinion, but also let her know in love what the Bible does say. His truth needs to be our bottom line on every issue, and every group discussion should reflect that.

PRAYERS FOR YOU!

May the Lord richly bless you for taking on the role of discussion group leader. Could I pray for you?

> *Heavenly Father, thank You for this child of Yours. Thank You for a willingness of heart to be used by You to touch the hearts of others, by Your grace and for Your glory. What a sweet sacrifice of service. I ask that You would shine special blessings in the group times and in every other place in the leader's life. May the leader come to know the group members in a deeper way and also know You in deeper ways. Father, I ask that lives would be changed by Your power. I ask that You would work right before the eyes of each discussion leader. I ask that even now You would be bringing in the group members whose lives You can touch through this forum. If there are those who don't know You, Father, please bring them in by Your Holy Spirit. Draw them to yourself. I ask that You would grant great wisdom for the leader—Your wisdom— and great insight into Your Word. Give leaders that amazing, Jesus kind of sacrificial love for each member of the group. Move and work, oh Lord—all praise and glory to You. Shine in every way. In Jesus' name, amen.*

DISCUSSION GUIDE

INTRODUCTION: ENLIGHTENING STRIKES

GET GLOWIN': Have you ever had a great idea that went oh-so wrong? Baking project? Home repair? Think about a funny lightbulb-over-the-head moment you could share that ended in something unexpected or chuckle worthy.

1. Look up the Ephesians 1:18–19 passage in several different versions and pick your fave. Write it on a card or sticky note and post it somewhere you'll see it every day.

2. Is there a change you'd like to see God make in your life? What do you think that change might require of you? Are you ready to do whatever it takes? Will you commit to stick with the lightbulbs study with everything you've got and let the Lord show you through His Word what He would like to do in you?

3. Pray through Ephesians 1:18–19, asking the Lord to do in you what Paul asked for the Ephesians. Praise Him for His mighty strength that makes it all happen.

Part 1: Lightbulb-Over-the-Head Enlightenment —Understanding the Real Light of the World

CHAPTER 1: GOD IS LIGHT

GET GLOWIN': Ever had one of those embarrassing gift experiences? Think of a time when you gave a gift you later discovered was on the embarrassing side of goofy. Or how about a time when you received one?

1. Write down some of the attributes and character qualities of God listed in this chapter and add others that come to mind. Why is it healthy and right for us to celebrate the God of light for who He is, for what He's done, and for what He will do? Celebrate Him through Psalm 145:1–5.

2. Have you ever looked to find the answers to life's questions in anyone or in any other place than in the God of light? What did you find when you looked elsewhere? What does it mean to find true enlightenment?

3. Does your concept of God line up with the word of God? Have you ever attributed aspects to the Father that were from your own thinking or from worldly philosophies and perceptions? How is life different when a person bases ideas of God on what others say versus on a life lived knowing the God of the Bible? What happens in your life as you celebrate Him more and as you understand more who He is?

CHAPTER 2: JESUS. THE LIGHT OF THE WORLD

GET GLOWIN': Have you ever missed something important by over-sleeping? Ever had anything interesting come from a time change you didn't see coming? Worst of all, have you ever had to deal with bad hair for a whole day as a result of a late start? Got pictures?

1. How would you describe Jesus' unique role as the Light of the world? What are some verses from Scripture that back up your description?

2. As you look through your description of Jesus the Light and the passages you've listed, how do you think these things change how we think, how we respond, how we live?

3. If you know Christ, what are some of the specific ways He's changed how you see people, how you behave toward them, how you handle your failures and shortcomings, and how and who you live for? Are you ready and willing to be changed even more? If so, write out your prayer of surrender to Him.

CHAPTER 3: YOU. THE LIGHT OF THE WORLD

GET GLOWIN': Have you ever experienced a minor injury that inter-fered with your usual routine in a major way? Share your most intense paper-cut kind of story. More serious injuries or illnesses? How did these impact your life and your perspectives?

1. God is light, Jesus is the Light of the world, and now we see we're also to be the light of the world. How do our "light duties" divvy out? Where do we get the know-how, the muscle, and the want-to? What Scriptures can you find to back up your answers?

2. Look at the Ephesians 5:8–20 passage at the end of the chapter. Make a list of life points you find in these verses—truths and instructions that change life. Keep it as a checklist for life for a week and then

evaluate to see how you've done on each point. See any changes you might need to make? Any thought processes that need tweaking?

3. What are some ways God is using you right now to shine His glory? How are you pointing others to Him? Do you think there may be other ways He desires to shine His glory through you? If so, what might they be and how can you accomplish them?

CHAPTER 4: THE LIGHT OF SALVATION

GET GLOWIN': If you could add an item to the "Rock, Paper, Scissors" game, what would yours be?

1. According to Romans 6:23, what have we earned? And what is the gift?

2. So what is the spiritual "covering" described in Psalm 32:1–2? Have you experienced that covering? If so, write out your "darkness to light" conversion experience. Ready to share? Every story, miraculous! If you prayed in the "What a Prayer" section of the chapter, giving Jesus your life, you've made the most important decision you've ever made—or ever will make. Heaven rejoices! Will you share it with someone today?

3. According to this chapter, you don't have to be perfect to follow Christ—since Jesus took care of our perfection need for us. But you do need to be willing to do something. What is that something? As you examine your life, how are you doing there? See anything that needs to change?

CHAPTER 5: LIGHT FOR LIVING

GET GLOWIN': Have you found any surprises in your microwave or your oven? How about the fridge? Share your laughable discoveries.
1. Did you look at the ugly list in 1 Peter 2:1–2? Write down each ugly item, then write what the opposite of each would be.

2. Is there anything ugly in your life you need to let go of? Ready to drop it and take a step back into the light?

3. According to this chapter, what are our weapons in fighting the battle that our fleshly nature wages against us? How are you personally wielding your weapons?

Part 2: Bright Ideas for Enlightened Living —Embracing the Light of Godly Living

CHAPTER 6: LIGHT THAT GIVES UNDERSTANDING

GET GLOWIN': What's your best diet story versus your worst diet story?

1. Why do you think godly wisdom is described as light? Does that influence your walk?

2. What is the "circle of wisdom" described in this chapter and where will it lead us? Controlled by wine or controlled by the Holy Spirit? What does each look like and how do they compare?

3. Pray through Psalm 119:129–35 making it your own personal prayer. Let that prayer shine through your entire week.

CHAPTER 7: GOD'S WORD GIVES US LIGHT

GET GLOWIN': Collect your best weird cat stories or funny cat pictures from the Internet. Can you find some funnies?

1. Romans 12:2 is a great verse of change. We're told to "not conform any longer to the pattern of this world, but be transformed by the renewing of your mind." How can we renew our minds?

2. This chapter lists seven ways you can box yourself in—in a good way. Are you ready and willing to get a little "boxy"? Read through

these every day for a couple of weeks and mentally check off the boxes each time. What a change God's Word can make!

3. Spend a few days making Psalm 119 a big part of your quiet time. Write down some of the things mentioned in this psalm that God's Word will do for you.

CHAPTER 8: PRAYING IN DE-LIGHT

GET GLOWIN': Any scary perm stories of smoking bangs in your past? Other hair disasters that still send a tingle down your spine?

1. Do you ever find yourself seeking all the right "feelings" and seeking self-interest more than you seek becoming a person who is full of faith? How does a person turn that kind of thinking around?

2. Have you ever chosen to pray bigger than your faith as the father in Mark 9 did? What happened?

3. The three "R" phrases in this chapter speak to the kind of attitude we're to have as we come to Him. Read through them every day for a week just before your prayer time. See any difference in your 'tude?

CHAPTER 9: BELIEVERS WHO REFLECT

Get Glowin': Got a gardening nightmare story? Or a story of glowing garden success? Harvest time!

1. Do you ever find yourself getting tired in your light walk? How does a person recharge?

2. How has God called you to reflect His light in serving others? Do you think He might be calling you to something new? How will you know? Look at the "outfit" He's called us to wear in the Colossians passage at the end of the chapter. Will you take on a challenge to let Him "clothe" you every day?

3. Are there people in your life that are a little more difficult to love than others? What is your duty toward them? How does your love for them affect how brightly you shine God's love?

CHAPTER 10: LIVING SAFELY IN THE LIGHT

GET GLOWIN': Got a bad poem in you? Go ahead, limerick away!

1. Have you ever had an experience that left you feeling like the Lord was far away? Where should we run in those times? Look again at Hebrews 13:5–6. Commit it to memory so that you'll have it handy at-heart to remind you of His presence, His love, and His eternal provision for you.

2. What are some practical ways you can delight in the safety of the presence of God?

3. Rejoice in the Zephaniah passage at the end of the chapter. Sentence by sentence, let its truths soak into your mind and your soul. Such comfort! Meditate on a phrase a day this week and see how the Lord might use it to change your week.

Part 3: Seeing Your Life Change—One Watt at a Time —Walking in the Light Requires Obedience

CHAPTER 11: STEERING CLEAR OF DARKNESS—SIN

GET GLOWIN': Got a memory of a favorite food gone tragically wrong? Feel free to insert ridiculous food fight story here.

1. What "things" do you think are the easiest for people to stumble over, spiritually speaking? What does it look like when someone treasures the things of earth and misses the treasure of heaven?

2. How does a person learn to choose well when it comes to resisting slipping back on those old paths of sin?

3. If you've never committed Matthew 6:19–21 to memory, consider making it one of your week's goals. What a great way to feed your mind the truth about real treasure.

CHAPTER 12: SOMETIMES THE KEY TO CHANGE IS...CHANGE

GET GLOWIN': What's the easiest change you've ever made? The most difficult? The most entertaining for others to watch?

1. Is there a change you felt the Lord wanted you to make that you found difficult? How did you overcome that difficulty and make the change anyway? What were the results? What about a change that's occurred in your life that you didn't get to vote on? How have you seen God work in it?

2. This chapter mentions that walking in His light requires a change in the way we think. What kinds of changes might those be? How do we surrender thoughts that sometimes seem out of our control?

3. How did you answer the string of "change" questions under the "My Consuming Prayer" section? What does it mean here to "encounter the Light"? How does that influence the answers to those questions?

CHAPTER 13: HOW MANY LIGHTBULBS CHANGE THEMSELVES?

GET GLOWIN': Most embarrassing photo of you. Willing to share? Willing to share someone else's?

1. Think of several examples of challenges people often face. Contrast and compare what each looks like with self-confidence versus

God-confidence. According to Acts 1:8, where should our power come from? How do we tap in?

2. Did you accept the challenge in this chapter to begin each day recognizing your need for His strength, confessing your dependence on Him? If so, how did it impact your day?

3. Look at the 2 Thessalonians passage in "A Little Extra Light for the Path" again. Chart it out into the things "asked for," the "results," and "how it happens." It's like diagramming life!

CHAPTER 14: LIVING IN THE LIGHT/ DWELLING IN HIS PRESENCE

GET GLOWIN': Can you think of a few things you've royally overdone? Care to share a couple of the most entertaining?

1. List practical ways we can make sure we're growing "more and more." The "more and more" verse is a great one to stick on your mirror or car dashboard for a few weeks.

2. Ponder the power of prayer as a key agent of change in living in the light and dwelling in His presence. What happens in our minds as we pray?

3. How can following in the light of Christ become the habit of life? In what direction are most of your habits leaning?

CHAPTER 15: UNFORGIVENESS BRINGS DARKNESS

GET GLOWIN': Do you have any ceremonial rituals similar to "The Grand Clipping of the Nails Ceremony"? Can you think of others that make you chuckle?

1. Is there an offense someone has committed against you that seems to keep looming over your day? Is it the kind of offense you should

rise above or is it the kind you should lovingly confront? How can you do either when you just plain don't feel like it?

2. Go through the chapter and list all the negative results of unforgiveness. Then list all the blessings of forgiveness. Wrap up your list with a passage of Scripture on the topic of forgiveness that most impacts you.

3. If there's someone you've yet to forgive, will you pray the suggested prayer toward the end of the chapter and get free? Will you commit to praying the prayer again anytime bitterness crops up again? Will you commit to putting down your grudge and picking up your cross?

PART 4: Watt in the World? —Living in the Light Gloriously Spills Over

CHAPTER 16: LIGHT-LIVING TESTIFIES OF OUR ALL-SUFFICIENT GOD

GET GLOWIN': Name your favorite dinner shortcuts. Is there a meal shortcut that had a not-so-tasty, laughable ending?

1. Write down some of the amazing things your all-sufficient God has done for you. Let your list feed a time of praise to the God of the universe, the source of all good.

2. According to this chapter, what happens when we encounter the all-sufficient God?

3. What are some practical ways we can be "glory placeholders"? Do you see yourself as a glory-reflector of His? How?

CHAPTER 17: LIGHT-LIVING CHASES AWAY OUR FEARS

GET GLOWIN': Is there something goofy that you once feared? Monsters under the bed? Fess up.

1. Have you ever seen fear take over someone's thoughts? Have you ever experienced it personally?

2. Talk about all the things light does. How do those physical properties of light relate to the spiritual things? What are the practical ways a person can get rid of fear?

3. Commit 1 Peter 5:7 to memory so it will be right in the front of your mind, ready to remind you to "cast" anytime fear threatens to overwhelm you.

CHAPTER 18: LIGHT-LIVING GIVES STRENGTH FOR EVERY CHALLENGE

GET GLOWIN': Are there some family legacies you would like to see pass on to the next generation? How about weird ones you're hoping to nip?

1. Are there stories of grace under pressure from family members or mentors in the faith—stories that the Lord has used to strengthen your own faith? What is it about that person's response that moves and inspires you to become all God wants you to be?

2. Does Paul's thorn bring to mind struggles you have faced or maybe struggles you're facing even now? How does his response move and inspire you to become all God wants you to be? How does it affect how you respond to your difficulty?

3. Read Psalm 18. Contemplate how big your "thorn" is compared to how big God's grace is. As you face struggles can you come to a place where you're willing to tell the Lord that you will endure the

struggle if it will bring glory to Him? Will you resolve that at any time you encounter hardship, you will lean hard on His grace?

CHAPTER 19: LIGHT-LIVING SHINES JOY IN EVERY CIRCUMSTANCE

GET GLOWIN': Ready for a cheesy-nacho party? What's your comfort food of choice?

1. This chapter touches on the joy we find in not settling for anything other than walking in His light—His way. What do you see people settling for in the world today? How do you suppose their joy level fares?

2. Describe the difference between a joy that makes you giggle and a joy that gives you peace—that joy that runs deep.

3. What counsel would you give to people who find their faith wavering in the dark times? What would you tell them if they're holding off following Jesus with everything they've got, waiting for the darkness to pass? How would you help them find assurance that the light is still there?

CHAPTER 20: LIGHT-LIVING INFUSES LIFE WITH HOPE

GET GLOWIN': What's the wildest baggage scene you've come across? What about the wildest bag?

1. Contrast the "hope so" kind of hope with the hope we focus on in this chapter. How does Psalm 33:22 apply?

2. Since Romans 15:4 connects hope and the Word of God, give your quiet time another evaluation. Are you treasuring the hope found in spending time with Him in His Word? Read Psalm 19:7–8 and underline each benefit of loving His Word.

3. How does a person share the living hope with others? Look at 1 Peter 3:15 again. How do we go about getting "prepared" as this verse instructs?

PART 5: Sanctified, Electrified! —Looking to the Light

CHAPTER 21: WORSHIP IN THE LIGHT

GET GLOWIN': What's the most extreme wake-up call you've experienced, alarm-wise? Got a funny wake-up story?

1. When was the last time you ignored your computer—email and all—and your cell phone for a few hours in a row? Would you accept a challenge to have a sort of "quiet diet," maybe even for an extended length of time? What would it take for you to set aside some uninterruptible time for the Lord?

2. What does it mean to worship in spirit and in truth?

3. We don't often think of our worship as "urgent." Can you think of reasons it could be described that way? Very specifically, what should our responses be?

CHAPTER 22: POWERING UP FOR LIFE

GET GLOWIN': What kind of crazy, mixed-up body game show can you come up with? Come on down!

1. What is the "mystery" referred to in 1 Corinthians 15:51?

2. According to this chapter, how do thoughts of the ultimate eternal change we have waiting for us in our future change us in the present? Of the three changes highlighted, which one seems to tug at your heart the most? Why do you think that is?

3. How do we wait for His coming "expectantly"? What does expectant waiting look like?

CHAPTER 23: DEALING WITH THE DARKNESS

GET GLOWIN': Got a "stepped in it" story? How about a picture of a not-so-picture-perfect moment?

1. When you encounter overwhelming darkness, where is the Father? How can you know for sure? Make your point(s) with at least two or three Scripture verses.

2. Do you know people who judge God's love and care by the circumstances they're experiencing at the moment? Why is this flawed thinking and how would you counsel them?

3. How does a person keep a tight rein on thoughts? List some practical ways to rein them in. What is referred to as a "great antinegative"? How does it affect your thoughts?

CHAPTER 24: LIMELIGHT VERSUS REAL LIGHT

GET GLOWIN': Ready to vent in another round of bad poetry? Topic: facial challenges. Do your worst.

1. How would you describe John the Baptist's "He must become greater; I must become less" way of thinking? How does that attitude reveal itself in a life?

2. Why do you think those secret places of hypocrisy interfere with our worship?

3. Look again at Proverbs 11:2–3, 20 in the Amplified Version shared in "A Little Extra Light for the Path." Make a list of the results of life on the pride side versus a life of humility. Spend time praying that God will ever-mold your ego to His delight.

CHAPTER 25: HEADLIGHTS ON YOUR OWN DAMASCUS ROAD

GET GLOWIN': What's the worst car you've ever driven? Do you have a funny car story or two?

1. What has impacted you the most through our look at the light of God and the God of light? What changes has He been working in your life? Praise time! Has the Lord brought you closer to those in your group? What have you learned about them? About yourself?

2. Is there anything keeping you from shining His love into your world? Fear? Feeling you have a lack of know-how? What can you do to overcome these obstacles and start getting the word out? Is there someone the Lord has placed on your heart—someone you know you need to share Christ with?

3. Are there other ways He's calling you to shine? How will you concretely share with others what the Lord has done in your life? Pray the prayer at the end of the chapter together, then go and glow!

Use the QR reader on your smartphone to visit us online at
www.newhopedigital.com

If you've been blessed by this book, we would like to hear your story. The publisher and author welcome your comments and suggestions at: newhopereader@wmu.org.

OTHER NEW HOPE BOOKS FOR WOMEN:

**How Can I Run a Tight Ship
When I'm Surrounded by Loose Cannons?**
*Proverbs 31 Discoveries for
Yielding to the Master of the Seas*
Kathi Macias
ISBN-13: 978-1-59669-204-6 • $13.99

The Friendship Factor:
Why Women Need Other Women
Brenda Poinsett
ISBN-13: 978-1-59669-247-3 • $14.99

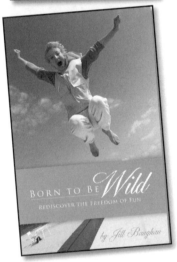

Born to Be Wild:
Rediscover the Freedom of Fun
Jill Baughan
ISBN-13: 978-1-59669-048-8 • $12.99

Available in bookstores everywhere

For information about these books or any
New Hope product, visit www.newhopepublishers.com.